## He Was Impossible to Second-Guess.

His hand stroked hers, and she pulled her arm away, whispering, "I thought you said you would behave!"

"Did I ever tell you I'm not very good about keeping promises when a beautiful woman is involved?"

"Well, I don't want your attention. I'm not looking for someone like you. You're not rich, and I won't settle for second best. I've had all that, and all it brought me was heartache."

Adam frowned, and a harsh mask descended over his face. "For your information, I only want to have a good time with a beautiful woman. I'm not interested in falling in love."

---

MARGARET RIPY
says that the support and encouragement of her fellow writers has been the most important influence on her first novel, *A Second Chance on Love*. She loves to travel and writes about the places she has been. Margaret writes every day "if only for a short time."

Dear Reader:

Silhouette Romances is an exciting new publishing venture. We will be presenting the very finest writers of contemporary romantic fiction as well as outstanding new talent in this field. It is our hope that our stories, our heroes and our heroines will give you, the reader, all you want from romantic fiction.

Also, *you* play an important part in our future plans for Silhouette Romances. We welcome any suggestions or comments on our books and I invite you to write to us at the address below.

So, enjoy this book and all the wonderful romances from Silhouette. They're for *you!*

Karen Solem
Editor-in-Chief
Silhouette Books
P.O. Box 769
New York, N.Y. 10019

# MARGARET RIPY
# A Second Chance on Love

*Silhouette* *Romance*

Published by Silhouette Books New York

**America's Publisher of Contemporary Romance**

SILHOUETTE BOOKS, a Simon & Schuster Division of
GULF & WESTERN CORPORATION
1230 Avenue of the Americas, New York, N.Y 10020

ISBN: 0-671-57071-4

First Silhouette printing April, 1981

10 9 8 7 6 5 4 3 2 1

*To my husband Luke,*
*without whose help*
*this would not have been possible*

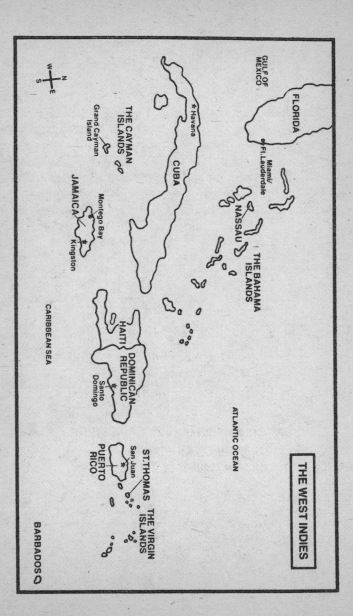

THE WEST INDIES

GULF OF MEXICO

FLORIDA

Miami
Ft. Lauderdale

★ Havana

CUBA

THE CAYMAN ISLANDS

Grand Cayman Island

JAMAICA

Montego Bay

Kingston ★

NASSAU

THE BAHAMA ISLANDS

CARIBBEAN SEA

HAITI

DOMINICAN REPUBLIC

Santo Domingo ★

ATLANTIC OCEAN

San Juan
★
PUERTO RICO

ST. THOMAS

THE VIRGIN ISLANDS

BARBADOS

N
W — E
S

# Chapter One

Shauna Peters's hands trembled as she reread the letter. She dashed the tears from her cheeks and tried to focus on the paper before her. The doors closed behind her and silence descended upon the courtroom.

Shauna, I am married.

She shifted in her chair, trying to digest those simple words.

"Mark, married," she whispered, a tear falling on the sheet she held. "No, it can't be! We're engaged!"

But the next sentence of Mark's letter jumped out at Shauna.

I married Catherine yesterday and we are leaving on our honeymoon.

Catherine? A vision of a sophisticated woman with long blond hair and large blue eyes filled Shauna's mind. A friend.

Shauna forced herself to finish reading the letter.

I am sorry to be writing to you, but I didn't know how to tell you in person. Catherine and I have been in love for quite some time, but fought our feelings because of our respect for you.

The word *respect* leaped out at Shauna. Is that all you felt toward me all these months while we were planning our wedding? she wondered.

There isn't anything I can say that will make this any easier, except that I hope one day you find someone that you can love as I do Catherine.

Love? But I have found someone—you, she screamed silently.

I am enclosing the two tickets for the cruise that we bought for our honeymoon. Catherine and I couldn't use them, but we want you to.

Sincerely, Mark.

Shauna crushed the letter between her fingers. Sincerely! Is that all I get after the years I thought were wonderful for both of us? she asked herself.

Shauna buried her face in her hands, the crumpled letter falling to the floor. The tears flowed.

A hand touched Shauna's shoulder. She jerked her head up and choked back her tears. She glanced over her shoulder as she wiped her cheeks dry with her hand.

"Shauna, you won the case. What's wrong? We were going to celebrate your victory." A tall woman towered over Shauna, a worried expression on her face.

Shauna pointed to the letter on the floor and said, "That."

The woman bent, picked up the letter, and smoothed the sheet. She scanned the paper, then looked down at Shauna. "Why, that creep!"

The tears threatened to return. Shauna bit her lower lip and stood.

"I can't believe that man! He sends you a *letter* here at the courthouse after your first big victory to explain he jilted you." The woman shook her head, her short red curls bouncing.

Shauna gathered her briefcase and purse and began to walk from the courtroom.

"Shauna, aren't you going to at least take these tickets?"

Shauna pivoted and stared at the woman. "I don't want them, Nancy."

"But you helped pay for them. You both saved your money for that trip. You deserve them . . . and more." Nancy picked up the folder with the tickets in them and offered it to Shauna.

Shauna hesitated.

"Think of all those months you two spent at your

9

apartment not going out so you could save your money."

"But I enjoyed those quiet evenings with Mark studying while I worked on my papers or wrote a summary for a jury. You know how I despise large parties."

Nancy thrust the folder into Shauna's hand. "The tickets are yours."

Shauna's fingers slowly encircled the folder. She stared at the red plastic that held the two tickets. Our dream, she thought and whirled around. She fled the courtroom and ran down the hall, ignoring the gawking people as she escaped into the ladies' room.

Shauna sank onto the sofa. She squeezed her eyes shut, but the images of Mark and her looking through all the travel brochures to pick the perfect honeymoon trip plagued her. She whipped her head from side to side, but the picture still filled the black void. As she brought her hands up to cover her face, she cried, "Stop it! Stop it!"

"Shauna! It's not the end of the world! He's only one man. There are a lot more men out there better than Mark." Nancy's harsh words accosted Shauna.

Through glistening eyes Shauna looked up at Nancy. "I loved him. Why did he do this to me?"

The question hung in the air. Nancy shifted from one foot to the other.

"Why?" Shauna shouted the word at Nancy.

"Because you have been too busy to see what was happening right under your own nose."

Nancy sat beside Shauna and continued. "Mark needs someone to pay all her attention to him. A career cannot be important to the woman who marries Mark.

Catherine is the type of woman Mark needs. She wants a home and a family with no thoughts of competing in a man's world."

"But I want a family, too."

"But you also want to be a good lawyer with a thriving clientele."

"I have gone to school for years with that purpose in mind. Mark knew that when we started dating," Shauna said.

"He thought he could change you—a mistake he realized before it was too late. Be thankful you two didn't marry. In time you'll agree with me that what has happened is for the best." Nancy stood. "Now for that celebration you promised me if you won."

Shauna forced a smile to her lips. "I don't feel like celebrating now."

"Nonsense. You've never gone back on a promise before. I won't let you now." Nancy tugged on Shauna's arm. Shauna rose and gathered her purse and briefcase from the floor.

"Okay. You win, but let's make it a short evening. I really do feel like getting to bed early."

Once Shauna was outside, she looked back at the courthouse. A feeling of pride surged through her. I won today, she thought. This is the beginning of a new life for me. But the feeling evaporated as she relived the moment the messenger delivered Mark's letter. A new life . . . without Mark. She frowned.

Shauna watched the city of New Orleans pass by in a blur as Nancy drove her sports car to the French Quarter. Thoughts of Mark bombarded Shauna's mind until she wanted to scream. She closed her eyes and listened to the sounds of the city—horns blaring, people talking—noises she tried to fill her mind with. But each time she would concentrate on a sound, her thoughts would slip back to the past—she and Mark playing touch football together in the park, going to the Top of the Mart and staying to watch the sun go down as night crept over the city. Shauna's heart twisted.

"No!" she whispered. Her eyes bolted open.

Shauna slanted a glance at Nancy, but her friend was maneuvering the car into a tight parking space. Shauna sighed.

When Nancy turned off the ignition, she looked at Shauna and said, "Let's have dinner at Antoine's."

"If you say so."

"Come on, cheer up. If we are going to spend a fortune for dinner, you should at least enjoy it." Nancy slid out from behind the wheel and slammed her door shut.

Shauna climbed out of the car and yelled over the top to Nancy. "You'll have to take me the way I am. You dragged me down here tonight. Remember, I wanted to go home and sulk by myself." Shauna grinned.

"That's better. We'll drown our sorrows in rich, fattening food."

Nancy headed for the restaurant with Shauna hurrying along beside her.

When they entered Antoine's, the headwaiter strolled toward them and asked, "How many?"

"A table for two," Nancy said.

They followed the man to a table set off to the side in the front room. Their waiter immediately brought them the menus, which Shauna studied while a busboy filled her water glass.

After ordering *pompano en papillote*, Nancy cut a

slice of French bread and buttered it. Popping a piece into her mouth, she said, "You know, you should go on that cruise and find yourself a man. Show Mark he isn't the only man in this world for you." Nancy took another bite of her bread and chewed it slowly. "Better yet, find yourself a rich husband to bring back to New Orleans. Money has always meant so much to Mark. Why do you think he even looked at Catherine in the first place? She is from one of the richest families in New Orleans. After he finishes medical school, he won't have any trouble getting started here or, for that matter, anyplace else."

Shauna stared at her plate. She recalled a conversation a month ago when Mark had said, "I want to be so wealthy we'll never have to worry about money the way my parents had to."

Why was I so blind to everything happening around me? Shauna wondered. But she knew the answer. I was too busy with my own life and problems to see what was happening to Mark and me. The too-late realization hurt. I've failed.

". . . but that hair of yours should be changed. Cut and styled."

Shauna looked up at Nancy. "What?"

"Shauna Peters, when I get through with you, you won't know yourself. I am going to make you over. You have beautiful large eyes with long black lashes that make the gray color stand out. Your skin is an olive tone unusual for someone with auburn hair. Boy, am I going to have fun doing you over for your trip." A gleam appeared in Nancy's hazel eyes.

Shauna laughed. "Hold it. You aren't going to do anything to me. I like the way I am."

"That's part of your problem. You have never cared how you looked. You always had Mark and, I might add, took him for granted. Did you ever take special pains to dress up in the latest styles, to go to a beauty parlor?"

"Well, no. I never had time. I was always working to pay for law school or going to classes," Shauna said, then looked down at her two-piece outfit. The gray suit seemed suddenly plain to her.

Dull, she thought. That's what my life has been. No excitement. Shauna straightened in her chair and stared at Nancy. Now *she* has had an exciting life—a newspaper reporter traveling all over the world to cover stories.

Shauna listened to what Nancy was saying. "Tomorrow we will go shopping and begin the campaign to change you into a butterfly—one who will snare a rich husband. No more work and worries for Shauna Peters if she doesn't want any."

Shauna smiled. The seed was planted. The idea grew. Beautiful. Rich. No cares or worries, she told herself. Excitement blossomed within her as she began to imagine herself differently. Not studying, working—but playing, laughing.

Shauna looked at herself in the mirror. Her eyes widened. Me? She shook her head. It can't be, she thought. She ran a finger across her cheek. She stared at her face, then turned to Nancy.

"What have you done to me?" Shauna asked.

"I have applied a little makeup to bring out your best features. I have emphasized your eyes because they are your prettiest feature. Here, let me show you again how I put the makeup on. You have to be able to do it for yourself."

"But you are coming on the trip with me, aren't you?"

Nancy's face twisted into a frown. "I've been meaning to tell you that my boss wants me to cover the Queen of England's visit next week. I can't go. I pleaded with him to send someone else, but he wouldn't." Nancy shrugged.

Shauna looked at Nancy in the mirror and said, "Then I'm not going. I need your moral support."

"Nonsense." Nancy waved her hand. "Now let me show you how to put your eye shadow on so a man will look into your eyes and drown himself in their depths."

Shauna laughed. "Don't be ridiculous."

But as she looked at herself in the mirror, Shauna could see how appealing her gray eyes were—so large, with a circle of long black lashes that made the gray seem almost silver. Maybe, she thought.

As Nancy applied a touch of rouge to her high cheekbones, Shauna glanced at the half-filled suitcase on her bed. "A whole new wardrobe," she whispered.

Shauna blushed as she remembered some of the revealing dresses she had bought. Will I ever find the courage to wear them on the ship? she wondered.

"Now lightly dust your face with this powder." Nancy handed her a compact.

After Shauna finished patting her face with the powder, she turned her face to each side and studied it. "I guess I'll get used to it. But Nancy, I have never worn very much makeup before."

"And you still don't have very much on. Just enough for the right effect. You know, you're a beautiful woman. With your hair cut and styled and with those new clothes, you are going to knock the men dead on that cruise."

Shauna fingered one of her auburn curls and said, "I do like my hair short and curly."

"Here, wear this comb in your hair on the right side behind your ear. I think it will be just the right touch for you."

Shauna placed the tortoiseshell comb into her hair, then examined herself again. "Yes, I like it." She stood and embraced Nancy. "Thank you, dear friend. I already feel like a new person."

"Send me a postcard from one of the ports. I know you will have fun. Remember that rich men dress to kill and stay in the large suites on the ship." Nancy walked out of Shauna's bedroom into the living room. "I'd better be going. You need your beauty sleep. Tomorrow is a long day." Nancy reached the front door. "Don't spend all night packing. And remember all the things I told you."

"Yes, Nancy. Be mysterious. Not too eager. Listen. Don't talk. Etcetera. Etcetera. I'm sure I will dream about all your instructions tonight. You know, Nancy, I did catch Mark at one time. I'm not totally a novice."

Nancy opened the front door. "See you next weekend. I'll pick you up at the airport."

"Okay. Bye, and thanks again." Shauna shut the door. The silence of the apartment overwhelmed her. She sighed. She looked through her bedroom door to the packing she still had to do.

"Oh well, I guess I'd better do it now or I'll be up all night." She walked into the bedroom and began to pull her new dresses from her closet.

She rubbed the shiny material of a topaz cocktail dress between her fingers. It feels so delicious, she thought as her skin tingled. After all these years of hard work, I certainly deserve to have some fun.

The image of a tall, dark, handsome man filled her dreams. She looked down on her left hand and saw the ring of pale skin around her third finger. Soon I'll be wearing a large diamond engagement ring that will hide the mark of *his* ring, she told herself. But her throat tightened as she thought of Mark.

Shauna shook her head. Love isn't for me, she thought. It hurts too much to be in love. Security will make me happy. But those words sounded hollow to Shauna as she finished packing her last dress.

# Chapter Two

The exhaust fumes of hundreds of cars and buses overwhelmed Shauna as she moved outside the Miami airport. She trudged across the pavement to the curb to wait for an available taxi. Surveying the throngs of people, she calculated her success at getting a cab within the next fifteen minutes.

She placed the two pieces of luggage down next to her and sat on one. Her arms ached and she rubbed her hands up and down them to loosen the sore muscles.

"What a day!" she whispered, as she withdrew a tissue from her purse and wiped her brow. All I need now, she thought, is to arrive at the boat with smeary makeup and frizzy hair.

Shauna smiled as she watched an old lady shove a man out of the way and clamber into a bus. By another bus, people were pushing others in front of them to hurry them along. They are all mad, came the thought as Shauna's chances of getting to the harbor on time became fewer and fewer.

Then she saw a cab pull up not three feet from her, empty. Before Shauna could scramble to her feet and grab her suitcases, she noticed a man barreling down upon the cab. She quickened her pace and stepped in front of the man as he was about to speak to the driver.

"I would like to go to Fort Lauderdale's port," Shauna said.

Behind her, she heard the man expell his angry breath. She tensed, waiting to be pushed aside.

The controlled words of the man held a note of amusement when he finally asked, "Since we are going to the same place, maybe we could ride together and split the cost?"

Shauna felt a twinge of guilt. She turned and looked into the face of the man. She stared at his deep blue eyes, so clear and captivating, then tore her gaze away from his eyes and replied, "That would be fine."

After loading their luggage into the trunk, they climbed into the cab. The driver maneuvered the car out into the traffic. Shauna felt the presence of the man next to her as she stared out her window. She shivered when she thought of the way he had looked at her. His penetrating gaze had seemed as if it had reached into her mind and probed her innermost thoughts. His deep, husky voice still rang in her ears.

"I'm Adam Steele." That throaty voice broke the silence that drifted between them.

Shauna turned and looked at him. She nodded slightly as she extended her hand and said, "I'm Shauna Peters."

He took her hand in his and shook it. The touch of

his flesh on hers tingled. She quickly withdrew her hand and held it in her lap. Her hands twisted together.

Nancy's words of advice sounded in her mind. *Don't be shy. Be bold and be interested in the men you talk to.*

Shauna swallowed hard, then asked, "Where are you from, Mr. Steele?"

A twinkle appeared in his blue eyes. He smiled, his two dimples almost making him seem boyish—almost, Shauna thought, but not quite.

"I'm from Dallas. And you?"

"New Orleans." The silence descended between them again.

Shauna watched the passing countryside speed by as they headed for the pier. The air felt electrified with tension.

She cleared her throat and turned back to face him. "What do you do for a living? Oil?"

He laughed. "I work at a factory, Miss Peters."

"Oh," was all she could think of to say.

"Not everyone in Texas works in the oil industry."

Shauna lowered her gaze and stared at her lap. "I realize that, Mr. Steele. It was just the first thing that came into my mind." A slow blush spread across her face.

She looked straight ahead. *Oh, that man!* She slanted a glance at Adam Steele and studied his dark features, the strong jawline, the way he wore his three-piece suit. *Handsome* flashed through her mind. But too arrogant, she told herself, and looked away.

When the cab pulled up in front of the pier where their ship lay at anchor, Shauna noticed the crowds of people hurrying from their buses and cabs into a building near the ship.

"I'll take care of the cab." He paid the driver, then turned to Shauna and added, "You can buy me a drink on the ship later."

Shauna fumbled in her purse. "I don't like to be in anyone's debt, Mr. Steele." She extracted her wallet and took out five dollars.

Mr. Steele's hand closed over hers as he said, "I'm in your debt for allowing me to share your cab. I probably would still be at the airport if you hadn't agreed." He smiled.

Shauna stared at his two dimples, then at their clasped hands. She pulled her hand back and replaced her money in her wallet.

"Very well," she mumbled.

As Shauna started to pick up her suitcases, Adam Steele gripped the handle on her larger piece of luggage. "I only have one piece and don't mind helping you carry yours."

"Mr. Steele, I can do without your assistance every time I turn around." Shauna jerked the handle of the suitcase from his grip and proceeded toward the building.

She heard his footsteps behind her, but tried to ignore the feeling that he was staring at her. The muscles in her back grew taut, the hairs on her neck stood out. She quickened her pace, blocking from her mind the weight of her luggage.

Fool, she told herself as she noticed the long distance she had to walk with her suitcases. You should have let him carry your luggage then write him off when you got on board the ship. Write him off! She laughed at the thought. Somehow I don't feel that will be easy to do.

When Shauna reached the line marked K–P, she

placed her suitcases on the floor and waited. While she moved slowly toward the head of the line, she shot a glance toward Adam Steele. He caught her look and flashed her a smile that made her blush and quickly avert her gaze. Again that feeling of being stared at enveloped her. She shifted from one foot to the other and fixed her gaze on the officer checking everyone's tickets in her line.

By the time Shauna handed the officer her ticket, her body was stiff with tension. She watched the officer tag her suitcases and then put them with other pieces of luggage on a cart.

He looked up at her and said, "Your luggage will be on board in a few hours outside your stateroom. If you have trouble finding your cabin, ask any of the crew stationed around the ship."

He gave her the ticket and turned to the next passenger. Shauna walked a few steps toward the gangplank and surveyed the area. She turned abruptly when a hand touched her arm.

"How about that drink now before we look for our rooms?" Adam Steele asked.

"I'm tired, Mr. Steele, and want to lie down before I unpack and check about my eating arrangements. Good day." Shauna walked away, her breathing shallow.

When Shauna stepped off the gangplank, her gaze darted to the sign MAIN DECK. She looked at her ticket. "Room 235 Atlantic Deck," she whispered, and headed toward a flight of stairs. She took out her map of the ship and checked her location. "Two flights down and to my right is my stateroom."

As Shauna placed her foot on the first step, she

glanced over her shoulder and, sighing, scanned the lobby. No Mr. Steele, she thought, and began to descend the stairs.

She reached the Atlantic Deck and walked halfway down the first corridor. When she thrust open the door to Room 235 and stepped inside, she examined the small cabin, taking in the two bunks with a nightstand between them, the closet, and tiny bathroom with a shower.

"Well, it isn't luxurious, but it will do. I don't plan on staying in this cabin very much anyway," she said aloud, and plopped onto the bunk. She kicked her shoes off, then eased down onto the bunk. Her taut body relaxed. She closed her eyes and sleep encased her.

The ship began to rock gently and she bolted upright in her bed. "We're out to sea," she whispered, and scrambled out of the bunk. Retrieving her shoes from under the other bunk, she put them on and opened the door to step out into the hall.

Hunger pains twisted her stomach into hundreds of knots. Why didn't I eat on the plane? she asked herself, but knew the excitement of the trip had been too much for her.

Must find out what table I will be assigned to, she thought, and made her way to the stairs. After climbing three flights of stairs to the Promenade Deck, she walked through the main lounge to the observation gallery, where she noticed an officer had set up his table. But an elderly couple was in front of the table talking with the officer. When they moved away, Shauna stepped forward and said, "I'm Shauna Peters. I would like a table assignment for my meals."

"Would you like to eat at the first or second seating?"

Shauna thought a moment, then said, "First seating." Behind her, she heard someone approaching the table. Turning, she caught a glance at Adam Steele, who flashed her a brilliant smile.

The officer was saying, as Shauna turned back to face him, "This is your table for the trip, ma'am." He handed her a slip of paper with TABLE NUMBER 17 on it.

"Thank you," she mumbled, and hurried away.

But as she was moving toward the door, she heard Adam Steele request her table and seating. Anger flamed within her and her face felt hot with rage. How dare he, she thought. I'll be so cold, he'll wish he'd never met me.

Shauna scanned the dining room before entering and approaching an officer. "Where's table number 17?"

The young man pointed across the room to a table in the corner. "Over there, ma'am."

Shauna smiled her thanks and walked toward the table with only one place empty.

As she started to pull the chair out and sit, Adam quickly stood and helped her into her seat. Shauna didn't acknowledge the chivalry but instead nodded to the two other couples at the table.

"I'm Shauna Peters."

"I'm Marshall Williams and this is my wife, Edna," an older man said.

"Nice to meet you," Shauna said as she turned her attention to the young couple next to the Williamses.

"Helen Morris," the woman said, her gaze glued to her husband's face.

The young man flashed Shauna a smile and said, "Tony Morris. We're on our honeymoon, so don't mind us if we seem absorbed with each other."

A laugh bubbled in Shauna's throat. "No, I understand." But she fought to keep the tears from billowing within her as she forced gaiety into her voice. Honeymoon. This would have been Mark's and my honeymoon, she thought, and stared at her plate.

She heard a deep, husky voice close to her ear say, "Shauna, I have a feeling we have gotten off to a bad start. May we start over? I'm Adam Steele."

The hairs on Shauna's neck stood out as a tingle ran up and down her spine. When she turned to face Adam Steele his bright smile melted her anger.

"Very well, Mr. Steele, we will start over."

"Please call me Adam."

He had begun to say something else to Shauna when the waiter brought them the menus. She examined the long list and decided on the lobster Newburg with a fruit salad and asparagus.

When the waiter came to take her order, she felt eyes boring into her as she talked with him. A slow blush washed over her face until her hands started to tremble and chills spread through her.

After the waiter moved on to take the young couple's order, she snapped her head around and stared at Adam. Through clenched teeth she said, "I don't like to have someone stare at me like I'm a spectacle."

Amusement lit his eyes. "Oh, I'm sorry. It's just that you are so beautiful. By far the prettiest lady on this ship."

Shauna's face felt as if it were on fire. She lowered her gaze and twisted her hands in her lap Words dried in her throat. He makes me feel so strange, she thought. Beautiful?

"Don't embarrass me. I'm hardly the most beautiful girl on this ship. Please, I thought you wanted to be my friend," she said in a bare whisper.

"Friend? Who said that?" He took her hand and said, "Much more than that, Shauna. I don't give compliments unless I mean them." Each word caressed her.

A frown narrowed Shauna's eyes. "No!" The word tore from her lips like an explosion. She looked up and glanced at each person at the table. Their gazes riveted upon her. Forcing a smile to her lips, she waited until they resumed their discussion between themselves before yanking her hand from Adam's grasp.

Blood pounded in her ears. She directed her gaze at him and said very slowly, *"Mr. Steele,* I do not care to be embarrassed by you ever again."

He took a sip of his water before saying, "That was your fault, *Miss Peters."*

Her mouth parted slightly as she choked back a retort. She straightened in her chair and concentrated on the food the waiter was serving. She smelled the freshly baked bread and the delicious odors of the main dishes as they were placed before each person, but her thoughts dwelled on Adam Steele. Why does he make me feel so foolish? Like a schoolgirl? she wondered. This trip isn't starting out like it was supposed to, Nancy. Where are the rich men?

Shauna surveyed each table and inspected the men. He's obviously with that woman. That one isn't rich. His clothes are too shabby. Ah, now he's nice-looking . . . but married, she said to herself. As she rejected one man after another, her attention was drawn to the captain's table. There, seated on the right hand of the captain, was a man who took Shauna's breath away. She exhaled slowly, then took a gulp of her water. The icy liquid eased the tightness in her throat.

Her gaze traveled over the tuxedo trimmed in black velvet that fitted his body perfectly. She took in his broad shoulders, curly blond hair, and deep brown eyes. Shauna swung her gaze to the seat next to the man and noticed another officer occupied that chair. Maybe he isn't married then, she told herself.

When she looked back at the man, she caught him staring at her. Her eyes widened when their gazes touched as if no one else were in the room.

For a long moment Shauna remained motionless. Then the captain said something to the man and the spell was broken. He looked away and in the confusion she dropped her gaze to stare at her food.

"Is something wrong with your meal, Miss Peters?" The waiter was standing next to Shauna. She looked up and said, "Oh, no. I'm just not very hungry."

Lifting her fork from the table, she pushed her food around on her plate, then nibbled some of her lobster. How can I meet him? Is he married? Who is he? Questions crowded her mind throughout the rest of the dinner.

As Shauna pushed her chair back after dinner, Adam leaned near her and asked, "Would you join me for a drink and watch the show with me? No more, I promise."

Shauna watched as the man at the captain's table left the dining room, then she said, "Yes, I believe I will, if you promise to keep it only on friendly terms."

Adam raised his hand palm outward. "I promise."

They made their way from the dining room, up the flight of stairs to the Lido Deck. When they entered the grand salon and bar, Shauna noticed that the place was already filling up with people. Adam steered Shauna to a table near the stage and pulled a chair out for her. She slid into it and placed her purse on the table. As Adam sat, a barmaid approached them.

"What would you like to order?"

Adam looked at Shauna. "I'll have a screwdriver," she said.

"Come on, Shauna, be more inventive than that. She'll take an Imperial and I'll have a Scotch on the rocks."

Shauna's heart pounded as she gritted her teeth together. "I . . . I do have a mind of my own and know what *I* like to drink, Mr. Steele."

"Mr. Steele again." He laughed.

The sound echoed in Shauna's ears. She moved to leave, but Adam gripped her arm and said, "Be seated. Don't make a scene here like you did in the dining room."

"I . . . I made a scene! How dare you—"

His hand gently stroked her flesh. She pulled her arm away from him and whispered, "I thought you said you would behave."

"Did I ever tell you I am not very good about keeping promises when a beautiful woman is involved?"

"I don't want your attention. I'm not looking for someone like you."

"Like me? Whatever do you mean?" Adam's eyebrows raised.

28

"You are not rich, and I will not settle for second best. I've had that and all it brought me was heartache."

"So I'm second best to you."

Shauna felt the cold edge to the man's words and shrank back. "What I meant is that I'm not interested in love, only security, which money will bring me."

Adam's brow creased as a mask of harshness descended onto his face. "For your information, I'm not interested in falling in love. I only want to have a good time with a beautiful woman whom *I thought* was intelligent. I'm now having my doubts about that." Adam shoved his chair back, threw some dollar bills on the table, then said in a tone barely above a whisper, "You obviously don't know how to handle the attention of a man. Your experience with men has been very limited. You take a lot for granted, *Miss Peters*. When you do find this rich man, one word of advice. Say very little to him. When you speak you give yourself away." He pivoted and walked from the table, his back stiff, his hands clenched at his sides.

Oh, what have I done? she asked herself. Shauna found herself wanting to shout after him, "I didn't mean what I said. That was Nancy's idea . . . not mine. Come back," but the words died in her throat.

*Isn't that what you wanted?* an inner voice asked. *Not to be bothered by him? He's not your type. Concentrate on that man at the captain's table. Nancy knows what she's talking about.*

Doubt invaded her mind as Shauna watched Adam's retreating figure. She remembered the brief flicker of hurt that flared within his eyes and winced at the memory. Maybe she does, Shauna thought.

Shauna stared into nothingness as her emotions warred within her. She started to rise from her chair, then plopped back down and squared her shoulders. No, I will not go after him. Good riddance, Adam Steele, she told herself. I'll show him and everyone else.

The waitress brought the two drinks. Shauna paid for them, then gazed at the tall glass before her with crushed ice and yellow liquid in it. She ignored the Scotch on the rocks, gripped her glass, and took a swallow of the icy liquid. Delicious. He was right about the drink. Guilt stabbed her at the thought.

"May I join you?" a deep low voice asked.

Shauna twisted her head around to look into the face of the man from the captain's table. He towered over her, a smile plastered on his face. Shauna returned his smile and nodded.

"I couldn't help but notice your friend's exit. I am David Powell." He sat in the chair next to her where Adam had been seated.

*Don't say anything to the rich man when you find him,* came the grim taunt. She pushed Adam's words to the back of her mind and said, "I'm Shauna Peters."

"I know. I asked the captain who you were."

Shauna's eyes dilated. "You did?"

"Yes, when I find someone attractive I like to know who she is." His brown eyes bore into Shauna.

She shifted in her seat and took another sip of her Imperial.

"Do I shock you, Miss Peters? May I call you Shauna since I think we will become quite close during this trip?"

Shauna swallowed hard. Nancy, you didn't prepare me for this, she screamed silently. Outwardly she smiled and said, "Yes, David. Your behavior is surprising only because it is different from the other men I have known in my life."

*Your experience with men has been very limited.* Adam's words crept into her thoughts again. No, it hasn't, she screamed within her mind, but her protest held no conviction. Shauna concentrated on the man before her. Maybe he's the one I'm looking for. Certainly not that Adam Steele!

"And where has that life been spent?"

"You mean to tell me you don't already know?"

"Give me a day and I'll know all about you, Shauna. I have my ways."

Shauna shivered. "I live in New Orleans."

"The Crescent City. I visit there a couple of times each year."

"Do you travel a lot?" Shauna asked.

"My business requires it from time to time."

"What is your business, David?"

His smile widened. "I own Powell Industries—in Chicago."

Shauna caught the proud tone in his voice. She slanted a glance at David Powell as she drank the last of her Imperial and noticed the arrogant tilt of his head, the strong jawline that bespoke authority. He would be a tough man to work for. The thought slipped into her mind and dwelled there as she mused about David Powell.

David moved his chair closer and leaned toward Shauna. "You haven't told me what you do with your time in New Orleans."

*Remember, be a mystery.* Nancy's words came to Shauna in a flash. She smiled to herself. But how with a

31

man like David Powell, who demands to know all about you and has the means to find out? she asked herself.

Shauna ran her fingers along the rim of her glass. "I'm a lawyer with the law firm of Mathers and Haas." She crossed then uncrossed her legs.

He released a slow whistle. "A lawyer?"

Shauna narrowed her eyes. He's mocking me, she thought. No, maybe he's impressed. But as Shauna examined the gleam in David's eyes, she shook her head. He's making fun of me. Her temper flared. She clutched her purse to her and started to leave.

"Mr. Powell, I'm not here for your amusement. Good night."

He laughed. "I'm sorry, but from the way you said it, I couldn't resist having fun."

She turned and looked him in the eye. She saw the amusement dancing in those brown depths and suddenly her anger vanished.

The band began to play as the cruise director appeared on the stage. Shauna eased back into her chair and focused her attention on the show.

David Powell whispered into her ear, "I must make it up to you for being so rude. Allow me to escort you to a nightclub when we reach San Juan Monday night. I know a marvelous place for dinner, then a floor show, before we hit the casino."

"That would be nice."

Thoughts of what to wear Monday night plagued Shauna throughout the show. She ignored the male singer and hardly noticed the magician's act. By the time the show was over, Shauna still hadn't decided what to wear.

When the last entertainer left the stage, Shauna

leaned back in her chair and sighed. Exhaustion seeped into every pore.

"I hear the band at the Pink Panther Club plays great disco music. Care to join me in some late-night dancing?" David asked.

Shauna suppressed a yawn and said, "I wish I could, but I'm very tired from the long day of travel. Can I have a rain check on that?" She offered him a faint smile.

"Not only can you, but let's make a date to meet at the club after the first show tomorrow night."

"That sounds fine. Till tomorrow night." Shauna stood.

"Good night, Shauna Peters." He touched her arm as she moved in front of him to leave.

She smiled and walked away as a chill invaded her body. Adam's angry face haunted her thoughts. David Powell's the type of man I need, she said to herself, not Adam.

# Chapter Three

Shauna eased into her chair and stared at the empty place where Adam had sat the night before. Guilt rose within her again at her rude behavior toward him. She shook her head. I owe him nothing, she thought.

But an inner voice said, *You aren't usually like that with anyone. Why, Shauna, with him?*

I don't know, she answered herself. Maybe he brings the worst out in me.

*Or maybe you want to like him, but he doesn't fit into Nancy's plans for you,* the inner voice said.

No! Shauna screamed silently. You're wrong. Shauna banished the thought from her mind and studied the breakfast menu. He will not ruin my breakfast or this trip for me.

The waiter appeared next to her with his pad and pencil. "I will have a glass of orange juice, a cheese omelet, some sausage, and a muffin, she said as she handed the menu to him.

Shauna's gaze traveled to the captain's table. Only the captain and one other officer were seated. She released a breath of air. After brushing her hair from her cheek, she leaned back in the chair. Her body went limp from the sleepless night. She closed her eyes and listened to the sounds of the dining room—the chatting voices of the passengers, the clinking of the dishes, the hum of the engines.

Shauna felt a presence next to her. Adam! Her eyes bolted open as she turned to look at him. Her shoulders slumped when she saw the waiter standing over her with her meal.

*Shauna Peters, you will call Adam after breakfast and apologize. You must settle this thing once and for all.* Her conscience invaded her thoughts again.

She smiled and straightened in her chair. Yes, that is what I will do, she thought, and began to eat.

With each bite of her breakfast she felt better and better. By the time the meal was over, she looked forward to the day. She pushed back her chair and rose. She walked toward the door and past the captain's table. She glanced at the place where David had sat last night. Her breath caught. David was talking to the captain, a cup of coffee sitting in front of him.

Shauna started to speak but noticed that they were deep in conversation. As she moved away from the table, her face felt hot at the way she had abruptly halted in the dining room near the captain's table waiting to be acknowledged by David Powell.

Was he ignoring me? she wondered. No, he didn't see me or he would have spoken. Shauna quickly pushed the thought to the back of her mind as she made her way to her cabin.

When she entered the cabin, she gasped. Everything was picked up and cleaned. "They certainly take care of your cabin when you're gone," she said aloud. She walked over to the bunk, sat down on the bed, and called information.

As Shauna dialed Adam's room number, her hand trembled. Licking her dry lips, she waited as the phone rang once, then twice. On the third ring he answered.

Adam's deep, husky voice sounded sleepy. "Hello, Adam Steele."

Shauna began to put the receiver back on the hook when she heard again, "Hello. Who's there?"

"Adam. This is Shauna. I'm so sorry I disturbed you."

"What time is it?" Adam asked.

Shauna could imagine him fumbling in the dark, trying to find a light to see his clock. "Eight," she whispered.

"What?"

"Eight o'clock!" Her voice was loud, too loud.

"I heard you the first time. I just couldn't believe you would disturb a guy so early."

"Early! Why, Adam, it is a beautiful day. You don't want to sleep the day away." She giggled. I won't let you bully me, she thought.

"If I remember correctly, Shauna, last night we didn't part on what you would say were good terms. I don't believe it would bother you one bit that you disturbed me or that I might sleep the day away." His voice was stiff.

"Adam, I'm sorry about last night. I really do want us to start out on better terms. Will you join me by the pool for a dip? I would like someone to talk to."

"And you think I'm available."

Shauna shook her head. "Oh, no. I'd enjoy your company. Please."

A long pause on the other end of the phone greeted Shauna's ear.

"When?"

"I want to go to the travel talk on San Juan at ten. So, say eleven at the bar by the pool?" Shauna kicked off her shoes and lifted her legs onto the bunk.

"You don't have to waste your time going to the travel talk. I'll show you around Old San Juan. I've been there before; then that night I'll take you to a restaurant I know about that serves great food."

"I can't. I have a date that night with David Powell." Now why did I tell him that? Shauna wondered. She gritted her teeth together.

"David Powell?" Another long pause stretched between them.

"I met him last night at the show."

"Shauna, do you know anything about this man?"

"What do you mean? How could I know very much? I just met him last night." I don't owe you any explanations, she thought, but fought the desire to say it aloud.

"I . . ." His voice faded into silence.

"Adam, are you there?"

"I'll see you at eleven, Shauna. Goodbye." He hung up quickly and all that was left was the dial tone.

Shauna stared at the phone for a long moment before replacing it on its cradle. Strange, she thought. He seemed like he wanted to tell me something. Oh, well. Knowing him, he just wanted to butt in and try to spoil things for me.

Shauna searched the faces of the poolside crowd. Adam stood at the bar in his bathing suit with a towel slung over his arm sipping a clear liquid in a tall glass.

Shauna walked over to him and said, "Hello." She smiled. "Have you forgiven me about bothering you this morning and for last night?"

He stood with a thoughtful expression on his face for a moment before answering, "I never seem to be able to hold a grudge for long." He flashed her a brilliant smile that sent a blaze through her body.

She wrapped her towel closer around herself. "Well, we have an hour before our seating for lunch. Where do we get our deck chairs?"

"I already rented them—one for you and one for me. Call it my apology to you for leaving so abruptly last night. That was wrong of me."

Shauna looked Adam in the eye. He doesn't say he is sorry very often, she thought.

"I accept. Now lead the way, kind sir." She bowed and swept her arm across her body.

A deep chuckle rolled from his throat as he strolled away from the bar toward a row of deck chairs near the pool. "Numbers fourteen and fifteen. There they are." Adam laid his towel on the chair, smoothed it over the wood, then lay down. He smiled up at her.

Shauna placed her towel on her deck chair and sat down. "Would you please rub some suntan lotion on

38

my back? I haven't been out in the sun much and would hate to burn the first day of my vacation."

He propped himself up on his elbow and said, "Fine. But are you sure you want me to touch you?"

She shot him a look over her shoulder. "Why not? I certainly can't do it alone. Someone has to help."

"Again I seem to be the one available for the job. I'm becoming a regular handyman around this ship."

Shauna twisted around. "Why do you always turn everything I say around to make it sound bad?"

He shrugged. "My cynicism, I guess." He took the bottle of lotion and squeezed some of the white liquid into the palm of his hand.

She stared at the lotion, stark white against the tan of his body. "You must work outdoors or at least spend a great deal of time outside."

"I sail a lot and play tennis. I like to keep in shape."

"What do you do for a living?"

"If you want me to put the lotion on your back, you had better turn around before this stuff dries in my hand." With his other hand he pushed her to face away from him.

Shauna jumped when he applied the lotion. "Oh, that's cold!" She tensed.

"Sit still." He laughed.

His fingers rubbed the liquid into her back. Her muscles began to relax as he massaged the lotion into her skin. She closed her eyes and breathed deeply. The salty tang of the air and the gentle swaying of the ship helped to relax her.

"There" broke through her daze of relaxation and brought her back to the ship and the man beside her. She took the bottle from his hand and applied the lotion to the rest of her body. Leaning back in her chair, she closed her eyes again.

They lay in the sun in silence. The sun beat down upon her until beads of sweat covered her body. Finally she sat up and looked over at Adam. "Care to take a dip in the pool? This heat is merciless."

He rose and helped Shauna to her feet. She ran to the pool, the deck scorching hot from the sun's rays. Gazing down at the clear water, she dove into the pool. The cool water enveloped her as she swam to the bottom, then started up toward the surface. She reached the top of the water and broke back into the sun. Shauna gasped for air and swallowed a mouthful of water. Water seared her throat, leaving a fiery trail. She coughed as she clutched the side of the pool.

"You didn't tell me this was salt water," she shouted to Adam, shielding her eyes with one hand. Shauna swam across the pool to where Adam stood and looked up into his laughing face. "I don't call burning one's throat funny."

"I'm sorry, but you didn't give me a chance to say anything to you. You hotfooted it over here so fast that you were gone from my side in a flash." Adam dove into the water and came up beside her.

She glared at him for a moment, then burst out laughing. "A lesson I'll never forget is always to check the water before you plunge into it. I could only think about how cool it looked and how hot I was." The water lapped against the side of the pool and splashed into Shauna's face. "I can't get over having waves in a pool."

Adam swam four laps, then pulled himself up onto

the side of the pool. He said as he extended a hand down to Shauna, "It is nearly twelve. Time for lunch."

Shauna grasped Adam's hand and let him lift her from the pool. "I hate to change into dry clothes. Let's eat on the Sports Deck. I hear they serve a buffet there."

"Sounds fine to me."

Shauna scurried to her deck chair and slid her feet into her sandals. As she watched Adam approach, she asked, "Doesn't the hot deck bother you?"

"Nope. I have tough feet, madam, like my feelings." A twinkle appeared in his eyes.

"I should know, I dented them enough in one day to last a lifetime."

"I have had far worse things said to me than what you said, Shauna. Don't think any more about it. Deal?"

"Deal." Shauna shook his hand, then gathered up her bathing suit cover. She slipped it on and started for the stairs. Adam walked beside her in silence.

They stood in line and filled their plates with assorted fresh vegetables and fruits. Shauna ordered a hamburger, while Adam made himself a sandwich from the cut meats on a platter. With their iced teas, they found themselves an empty table and sat down.

As Shauna was popping the last bite of her hamburger into her mouth, she saw David Powell stroll from around the corner toward the bar. He ordered a drink, then began to talk to a woman beside him. Jealousy swelled within her. She diverted her gaze and caught Adam staring at her.

"David Powell?" he asked, in a low tone.

Her eyes widened. "How did you know?"

He grinned. "From that predatory gleam in your eyes."

Shauna's gaze wandered to David Powell, his back facing her as he leaned close to the tall, willowy woman in a brief bikini. Shauna sucked in her breath before turning to face Adam again.

Adam quickly lowered his gaze and masked the expression that held his eyes. He toyed with the last bit of his fruit before saying, "So, this is your rich man that will solve all your future problems." His voice was a level above a whisper. Shauna strained to hear what he was saying over the chatting of the people around them. He looked up and their gazes locked. Frustration edged its way into Adam's blue eyes.

Shauna swallowed hard and glanced away. "No . . . I mean yes," she mumbled.

His soft voice cascaded over Shauna as he spoke. "I feel sorry for you, Shauna Peters. You don't need money."

Shauna met his observance. "You don't know what I need, Adam Steele. Money is safer than love." She could feel the tight smile spread across her mouth.

"Perhaps you are right. I won't try to run your life for you." He paused, as if searching his mind for something, then he said, "This morning, as I was looking at the newsletter they send out every day, I noticed they will be showing the movie *Murder at Sunrise House*. I love to watch a good mystery. Would you care to join me this afternoon at the movie theater?"

"That sounds great. Whenever I get a chance to read, it is always a mystery, and Seth Taylor is one of my favorite authors. I hope they handle the movie well.

Sometimes you can hardly recognize a book when it is made into a movie."

"Have you read *Murder at Sunrise House?*"

"No. Lately I haven't had much time to do anything except work. Being a new lawyer with a firm can require a lot of hours if you want to become successful."

"And I suppose being a female doesn't help you?"

"Being a female has nothing to do with whether I am a good lawyer or not. My firm believes the same way as I do about the sex of a lawyer."

Adam raised both hands and said, "I give up. You've got me. Don't shoot."

Shauna laughed. "You can always get me angry at you. No more talks about the female role in society. This is a vacation."

"I quite agree, and if we're going to enjoy the sun we'd better get back to the serious business of getting a suntan."

As Shauna scooted her chair back, her gaze darted to David, standing by the bar. At that instant he looked at her and smiled. She nodded and quickly diverted her gaze to Adam. Let him wonder who I am with, she thought. Two can play the game.

Shauna took Adam's hand and followed him away from the bar. She felt David's stare move with them. Her hand gripped Adam's tighter until he stared down at her and said, "I believe you caught your rich man's attention. However, I only have two hands. Please don't squeeze the life out of this one."

Shauna made her way into the center of the row of seats. She heard Adam curse softly behind her as he stumbled and hit the arm of a chair. Darkness shrouded her smile as she pictured Adam's face when the curse exploded from his lips.

She whispered over her shoulder, "It was your idea to sit in the middle. If I remember correctly you said those were the best seats in the house." Her laughter rolled from her throat.

She heard his sudden intake of breath and brought her hand up to her mouth to suppress her laughter.

Halting halfway into the row, she asked, "Is this all right for you, Adam?"

"Fine," he growled, and fell into the seat next to hers.

As she eased into her chair and leaned back, the movie began, the credits rolling across the screen.

As scene after scene played on the big screen, Shauna found herself gripping the arm of the chair in terror. An icy shroud covered her. When the murderer lunged out from behind a door, Shauna screamed. Adam cuddled her to him, his hand pressing into the skin of her upper arm. She moved closer to him as the tension of the story built. She grabbed him and held on to his arm. When the last scene of the film passed from her view, she eased the crush on his arm and pulled away from him.

The house lights suddenly flooded the room. Shauna blinked at the momentary brightness. When she looked into Adam's face, she tensed. She saw a flicker of passion slip across his features to be replaced with a neutral expression.

Her heart pounded against her ribs. Just the excitement of the movie, she told herself, and forced a cheerfulness into her voice as she said, "I hope you can manage to leave the theater as gracefully as you entered."

"I believe that man over there deliberately tried to trip me." Adam pointed to a short, skinny man with a bald head.

"And succeeded from what I heard."

"I have to eat dinner at the same table as you tonight." He straightened. "I have big shoulders. I can take anything you fling at me. Go ahead." He patted his shoulders. Shauna saw a sparkle appear in his eyes that made them glisten like diamonds. They both broke out laughing as they left the theater and stepped into the corridor.

"Speaking of dinner, I only have thirty minutes to change for tonight." Shauna wiped the tears of laughter from her cheeks.

"You look fine. You don't have to dress up for dinner." Adam's gaze wandered down the length of her ever so slowly.

"Oh, yes, I have to. I have a da——"

"A date. You can say the word around me. It won't ruin my evening, Shauna. As a matter of fact, I have plans to enjoy this evening, too. Maybe we'll run into each other. I'll walk you to your cabin." He took her hand.

Shauna stared at their clasped hands. "I can find my way back to my cabin alone. You don't have to come with me." Confused as his thumb drew slow circles in the palm of her hand, words rapidly formed in Shauna's mind and spilled from her lips. "I know it's a big ship, but . . ."

Adam pressed a finger to her mouth. "Shh. I know you're a big girl and can find your own way back to your cabin, but where I come from, ma'am, a guy escorts a gal home after they've had a date."

"A date! We just met at the movie theater, that's all." She felt the strength flow from her legs. A wild, shaky excitement pulsated through her veins, reaching every part of her. She tried to pull her hand from his before she collapsed against him, but his hold tightened.

He tucked her arm through his and began to walk. "Do you still want me to show you around Old San Juan tomorrow afternoon?"

"Yes."

"We'll see the fort, then do some shopping. You always have someone back home you feel like you should buy some gift for."

Back home, Shauna thought, a sigh escaping her lips. In the last twenty-four hours I had succeeded in forgetting Mark. Maybe this trip will benefit me even if I don't find a rich husband.

"Yes, I do have to get a few gifts for some friends. Do you have presents to buy for family or friends, Adam?"

He laughed. "Perhaps, a few."

"The man of mystery."

"Not really. It's just that my life history would be boring to you."

Shauna halted at her door and leaned against it. "I

46

think all that traveling yesterday is catching up with me. I'm tired."

A smile brought laugh lines to the corners of his eyes. Shauna stared into their blue depths, a tightness in her throat.

"It has been a rather long day and we still have the evening ahead of us. But then, when you start it earlier than planned . . ." He shrugged, amusement lighting his eyes.

She lifted a hand, palm outward, and said, "I swear I'll never bother you again before eleven."

"I expect you to hold to that promise."

"My promises are better than yours."

He placed his arms on each side of her and leaned closer to her. His blue eyes became intense, darker. "Your lips are begging to be kissed, Shauna." Her name was a husky whisper.

Move, she told herself, before he . . .

She tilted up her chin and opened her mouth to speak. His mouth descended upon hers and smothered her protest. When his arms gathered her to him, all thought of resistance fled from her mind. His tongue darted into her mouth, plundering, tasting. She wound her arms around him and returned his kiss with her own hungry one. He ran his hands up and down her back in a slow, rhythmic pattern that was quickly drawing the strength from her.

*No! I don't want this!* Desperation worked its way through her. Her breathing grew shallow, labored, as she drew away from Adam.

"No! Adam, please!"

Shauna turned, yanked her door open, and escaped

into her cabin. The sound of his curse penetrated the quiet. Sinking onto her bunk, she gripped her trembling hands together and touched her lips as a tear slid from her eye.

"I *can't* fall in love with him. Love hurts so much! I don't want to feel it again."

# Chapter Four

Shauna stood by the railing at the bow of the ship and felt the wind lashing at her. Its roar screamed in her ears as she watched the ship glide through the water toward the port of Old San Juan. She scanned the rocky shoreline and saw the fort to her left. That must be what Adam wanted to show me, she thought, and inspected the fortress that stood at the entrance to the harbor.

Shauna ran her tongue across her dried lips, tasting the salt of the sea. She breathed gulps of the tangy air, then released it through pursed lips. An invigorating feeling washed over her as she took in the sights of the city. Old buildings surrounding the harbor caught her attention and held it.

She jumped when someone touched her arm. Twisting around, she faced Adam.

"I love the sea," she said and turned back to look at the city as the ship was maneuvered into its berth.

"I know. It's fresh, alive."

Adam stepped next to her along the railing and leaned on it. Shauna slanted a glance at his face as he examined the area. His features were intense, but for the first time Shauna noticed a gentleness there, too.

Her face flamed as she remembered his kiss. She touched her lips and relived the pressure of his mouth upon hers. Even with the sun beating down upon her, she felt chilled. She shook the thought of Adam's kiss from her mind and concentrated on Old San Juan.

She watched as the sailors secured the ship to the dock. "Do you think it will be long before we can leave the ship?"

"Not very long. They're connecting the gangplank with the ship now," Adam said.

"Good, let's get to the Promenade Deck and get in line." Shauna tugged on Adam's arm.

"Okay. Okay. The city isn't going anywhere. It will still be there in thirty minutes."

"But I want to see as much as I can of it in the short time we have." Shauna pulled Adam along the deck toward the stairs.

When they arrived at the debarkation area, Shauna glanced over her shoulder and said, "We won't even have to get a taxi. The city is right outside waiting for us."

Shauna noticed people were already gathered by the door waiting for the sailors to drop the ropes and open the sliding doors. Shauna and Adam stood near the front of the crowd. She shifted from one foot to the other as the minutes ticked away. When Shauna started for the stairs, the two sailors stationed at the ropes moved everyone aside en masse. Shauna turned and pushed her way back to Adam. He grasped her hand and they were pulled along with the mass of people leaving the ship.

Shauna and Adam walked down the gangplank into a building. They browsed through one of the shops in the building before descending to the ground floor and the street outside.

She looked at several narrow streets that ran down to the harbor, then at Adam. He pointed to the middle one and said, "Let's walk up that one first. There's a jewelry shop I want to show you." He gripped her hand tightly and they ran across the street.

"Have you taken this cruise before, Adam?" Shauna asked, panting to catch her breath when they reached the other side of the street.

"No, once I traveled here for my company. That was a couple of years ago, so I hope the shop is still there." He began to stroll away.

Shauna rushed after him. "Slow down. My legs aren't as long as yours."

"I thought you wanted to see everything before dark. We can't stand around on a street corner and discuss unimportant things if you do." His lips curled into a smile that didn't touch his eyes.

Adam slowed his pace and Shauna walked beside him up the street two blocks. He halted in front of a shop halfway up the third block and said, "This is the place. Let's go inside."

Shauna took a tissue from her purse and wiped her brow. When they entered the shop, she felt cool air rush over her.

"I might stay here the rest of the afternoon. It's so *hot* outside. When you're on the ship the breeze is always keeping you cool, but on land it's another story."

"You should be used to it by now. New Orleans is very humid." Adam walked over to a salesclerk and spoke to her. "I would like to look at your selection of diamond rings with just one large stone."

Shauna suddenly lifted her head and darted a glance at the case the woman was showing Adam. She saw Adam shake his head at several rings.

"No, none of them is what I want. Thank you."

As Adam turned around, Shauna quickly looked back at the tray of bracelets in front of her. She heard his footsteps approach her. Ring? Who is it for? she wondered.

"Did you find anything you wanted?" he asked.

She blushed. "Well, no, not yet. I've just started to look."

Adam stood by Shauna as she fingered first one bracelet then another. She ran her fingertips across the rest of the jewelry before facing Adam and saying, "I've seen all that I care to see. I think I'll wait until we reach St. Thomas to buy any presents. The cruise director told us at the talk yesterday that St. Thomas has the best buys of all the ports we visit."

Adam guided Shauna from the shop. "Where would you like to go?"

"Let's just walk. We can visit the fort on the way back to the ship."

As they strolled further up the hill, Shauna said, "Maybe you'll find what you are looking for in St. Thomas, too."

"Perhaps," he whispered, half to himself.

They walked in silence. Shauna window-shopped as they passed store after store of clothes, jewelry, pottery, and exquisite art objects.

Halfway up the hill, Shauna stopped at a street vendor's stand and bought a small banana. As she was peeling the outer skin away, she felt something yank at her arm. She whirled around as a man cut the straps of her purse and began running down the street. Shauna screamed. Adam pivoted and glanced first at her, then at the fleeing man.

With lightning-quick speed Adam raced after the thief. Shauna felt her breath trapped in her lungs as she watched Adam gain on the man. When Adam was within two feet of the thief, he leaped and plunged into the man. They tumbled to the pavement. All Shauna could see were arms and legs flying in all different directions until her purse was knocked away from them.

Shauna rushed down the hill toward the scuffling pair. She was within a couple of yards when she saw the thief break from Adam's hold and scramble away. Shauna grabbed her purse and hugged it to her. She looked up to see the man run from the gathering crowd and disappear around a corner. Adam bolted to his feet and started after him.

"Don't go, Adam!" Shauna shouted. Her voice shook with her fright.

Adam halted and spun around. He covered the distance between them in three long strides. His arms encircled Shauna's trembling body and drew her close to him.

"You're all right now," he whispered against her hair.

Shauna's heart hammered against her breasts. Her lungs ached. She nestled within the circle of Adam's arms for a moment while her heartbeat slowed and she took deep swallows of air.

"Oh, Adam, that knife was within inches of my skin." A picture of the gleaming silver of the blade filled Shauna's mind. She shivered.

"I think we have seen enough of the city. Let's go back to the ship and have a good, tall drink. I think we both could use one."

Adam placed his arm around Shauna as they walked back to the ship. Thoughts of Adam fighting the thief occupied Shauna's thoughts as she put one foot in front of the other. Her body moved automatically, apart from her mind.

Shauna released a sigh when they boarded the ship. She felt her taut muscles loosen while they walked toward the lounge.

Adam directed her to a table and sat down. He stared up at her and asked, "Aren't you going to have a seat?"

Shauna saw the amusement deep within his eyes and shrugged. "Yes."

Shauna could see his battle of will to keep his mouth from turning upward as she sat next to him.

"I'll say there are some advantages to being with a female that believes she's an equal to a male in all respects. Not as much work for the man on a date."

Shauna observed the smug smile that spread across his mouth and bit back her retort. She smiled and said sweetly, "I think I'll have an Imperial. It's a delicious drink."

Adam arched one eyebrow.

"Okay, I admit you were right . . . *but just that one time.*"

Adam signaled to a waitress, who walked over to the table. "An Imperial and a Scotch on the rocks." When the waitress left, Adam turned with a serious expression on his face and asked, "Are you all right?"

"I never had that happen to me before. I don't know what I'd have done if I had lost my purse. All my money is in it." Shauna touched her purse at her side.

"A word of advice. Put at least half of your money into a safety deposit box at the purser's office. I know you carry traveler's checks, but it's still a hassle to have them replaced."

The waitress placed their drinks on the table, and Adam paid for them.

Shauna took a sip of her drink. "I'll do that the first thing tomorrow morning. I'm sure it's too late to do it now." Shauna looked at her watch and exclaimed, "Oh, no! I'm going to be late for my date." She scrambled to her feet. "I had a nice time this afternoon aside from what happened at the end. Thanks, Adam. See you."

Shauna hurried from the bar and down the stairs to her cabin. She flung her clothes off, stepped into the shower, turned the cold water on, and let the icy water pummel her body.

When she finished, she dried herself quickly, then slipped on her underwear. "Now to decide what to wear," she whispered.

As Shauna inspected her wardrobe, she fingered a red dress. The fight earlier that day invaded her thoughts again. You didn't think twice, Adam, about going after that man, she thought. Would Mark have ever done that for me? No, he would have said that I should contact the traveler's check bureau and get my checks replaced. Shauna laughed aloud, no amusement in the sound.

She touched the shiny material of an olive green gown and said aloud, "This should do the trick. David will certainly notice me tonight."

Pulling the dress from its hanger, she laid it on her bunk and stepped back to examine it. Color fanned across her cheeks as she scanned the dress with its plunging neckline and a slit on each side.

Shauna slid the gown down her body and felt the soft material cling to every curve. She turned sideways in front of the mirror, ran her hand across her flat stomach, and smiled. "Not bad," she whispered, and sat in front of the mirror to apply her makeup. She accented her eyelids with green eye shadow and darkened her eyelashes with black mascara. After putting on a touch of rouge and powder, she leaned back in her chair and said, "That should make you proud of me, Nancy. I did everything you told me to do." Shauna brushed her short curls away from her face, turned her head to each side, and put the tortoiseshell comb behind her right ear.

She was gathering up her compact and money to place in her purse when a knock sounded at the door. She dropped her money on the bed, the knock startling her.

"Just a minute," she called out, and quickly finished

filling her beaded purse with her money and compact. Turning toward the mirror, she put some lipstick on before walking to the door and thrusting it open.

David Powell leaned against the door frame, a look of boredom on his face. His brown eyes lit up when he saw Shauna. He released a slow whistle and said, "You're lovely, Shauna."

"I hope the delay was worth it," she said as he took her arm and escorted her down the corridor.

"Well worth it." She felt his grip tighten on her arm.

David bent across the arm of his chair and whispered into Shauna's ear, "I don't think I have been out with anyone who blushes as lovely as you do."

"You'd think being from New Orleans I'd be used to this type of show, where women wear little or nothing, but I still get embarrassed." Shauna felt the color in her cheeks heighten even more as a woman with only a G-string on strutted past her on the stage.

David threw back his head and laughed. Shauna felt the eyes of the people around them staring at David and her. Her face burned and she took her program and fanned herself. She glanced at her watch. Only fifteen more minutes and we can leave, she thought, and stared at the second hand as it went around three more times before she looked at the dancers on the stage. The women kicked their legs high one final time before the curtain fell.

A magician appeared before the closed curtain on the stage and began a trick. Shauna sat mesmerized by his quick hands. As he finished his last stunt, Shauna looked at her watch and sighed. Four minutes to go!

She watched the women stroll out onto the stage for

the grand finale, their fans waving. You're a prude, Shauna Peters, she told herself. You're looking at nothing you haven't seen before. Why this embarrassment? The answer came to Shauna in a flash—David Powell. I hardly know this man. He says all the right things, but still . . .

The lights flooded the room. Shauna leaned back in her chair and relaxed. She noticed people beginning to leave, but David sat still in his chair and took another sip of his drink.

Shauna stared at her empty glass. When she looked up at David she caught him studying her. She felt color again flood her cheeks.

"Do you get embarrassed easily, Shauna? Or is it because I make you nervous?"

Shauna swallowed hard. "Both," she murmured.

He laughed. "Someone who tells the truth. This has been a refreshing experience, going out with you."

"Are you making fun of me? I get the feeling sometimes you are." Shauna leveled a penetrating look at him.

A frown narrowed his eyes. "No, Shauna, I'm not making fun of you. Most people are to laugh at but not you, my darling. You are too different. You are one of the few people I've met lately who knows how to tell the truth." David gripped her hand within his. "That's rare in today's society." His brown eyes grew dark with emotion.

"Well, David Powell, I was promised a night spent at a casino. Show me the way. I'm ready to lose my well-earned money." Shauna rose and extended her hand for him.

He's like all men, she thought as they walked from the nightclub, across the corridor, and into the casino. He just needs a good woman to make him happy. And I am that woman. Shauna beamed with excitement.

She surveyed the glistening lights and crowds of people standing about gambling or watching others lay their bets. She moved with David to the one-hundred-dollar blackjack table. David sat while Shauna stood to his side. He placed a thousand-dollar bill on the table. The dealer gave him ten chips. Shauna's eyes grew rounder when David laid his first bet, three chips in front of him.

As the pile of chips by David grew, Shauna looked around the room. Her gaze rested on Adam, sitting at a blackjack table across from her. She smiled when he glanced up and saw her. He waved before resuming his concentration on the play of cards before him.

"I think I'll find a table to play at. This is a bit steep for my means," Shauna whispered into David's ear. He nodded, and she walked around the tables looking for an empty chair at one of the five-dollar blackjack tables.

Throngs of people waited their turn to sit at one of the less expensive tables. Shauna scanned the crowded tables, sighed, then wandered over to the slot machines and placed a quarter into a slot. The tumblers rolled. An orange locked into the first place. The second spun to a halt with an orange showing. Shauna felt her heartbeat accelerate. The third slowed. Shauna saw flashes of orange speed by. The third tumbler clicked off and an orange fell into place alongside the other two. Shauna watched as quarters gushed from the mouth of the machine. A small gasp escaped from her throat as the pile of quarters grew in the tray. She stared at her winnings and felt elated.

"I've never won before," she said to the man next to her. She scooped the quarters into her purse and walked away, the weight of the purse feeling good on her shoulder.

Shauna spied an empty place next to Adam and scurried to the chair. She slid into the seat as an elderly gentleman was about to sit down. When he glared at her, she flashed him a smile.

"You certainly have a way of slipping in front of people. But then if you didn't I might not have ever found you on the ship. Going to try your luck at blackjack?" Adam asked.

"I just won ten dollars at the quarter slot machine."

Adam pursed his lips and whistled. "You might break the bank before the night is over."

"I don't see you doing very well." Shauna pointed at the small stack of chips by Adam.

"A run of bad luck, but now that you're here I'm sure that will change."

The dealer gave each player one card face up, then himself one face down. As he dealt the second card, Shauna received a jack while Adam got a four. She stared at her jack and two of clubs. What to do? she asked herself. Looking at the dealer's cards, she saw only a king. When the player next to her busted, Shauna swallowed hard and asked for a card. The dealer flipped over a two of hearts.

She smiled and said, "Hit me again." A seven of clubs fell next to her two.

"Twenty-one," the dealer said, and moved on to Adam.

Shauna watched Adam receive two more cards, totaling nineteen. The dealer then turned his other card over to reveal a three. He slid a card from the box and flipped it over. A king.

"Twenty-three. Dealer pays player number one, four, and five." The man stacked an equal number of chips in front of Shauna as she had placed there.

"See, I told you my luck would change. You dazzle the cards, love," Adam said and pulled in his chips.

"Then I expect a cut of your winnings."

"Will you share my loss with me since you're so rich now?"

Shauna leveled him a withering glance, then straightened in the chair and left the bet there. As she won the next round, she squealed with excitement. "I won again."

"See that man over there?" Adam gestured toward a man behind the table, wearing a black tuxedo. "The manager seems awfully interested in you. Either he thinks you're going to win big with those five- and ten-dollar bets"—Adam leaned closer and whispered into her ear—"or he thinks you're the most beautiful woman in the room and he can't keep his eyes off of you."

Shauna gathered up her chips and slid off the stool. "It's impossible to concentrate on the cards, Adam Steele, with you sitting next to me and making those ridiculous comments. I hope you lose your shirt." She turned and scanned the crowd for David. She caught sight of him and smiled.

David approached her. "I see you have won, Shauna." He waved his hand toward the chips she held.

She turned and exclaimed, "Can you believe this?" Shauna felt her face light with her excitement. "I've never won anything in my life and now I have thirty dollars here!" She snapped her purse closed and started for the cashier.

At the window she dumped the contents of her purse on the ledge and pushed the chips through the opening to the cashier.

The cashier counted out three crisp ten-dollar bills and shoved them through the opening toward Shauna. She stared at her winnings for a moment before picking the money up and stuffing it into her purse.

"We'd better head back to the ship before we're left stranded," David said, and took Shauna's elbow to guide her from the casino.

David hailed a taxi outside the hotel. He helped Shauna into the cab, then slid into the back seat after her. Shauna placed her purse in her lap and looked out the window at the passing lights of San Juan. They traveled along the highway from the newer part of San Juan into the older section of the city in silence. As they approached the harbor, Shauna felt David's arm slip across her shoulders. He pulled her closer to him.

"I had a wonderful time tonight, my darling," he whispered against her hair. "I don't want the evening to end."

Shauna stiffened.

He laughed. "What I mean, my little girl, is that I want to watch the ship leave San Juan with you at my side." His fingers massaged her upper arm.

Shauna felt the breath rush from her lungs and went

limp as she listened to his soft laugh. "I would love to, David."

The taxi halted in front of the building where the ship was anchored. David paid the driver, then led Shauna up the stairs to the gangplank. She noticed other couples drifting back to the ship arm in arm. David laid his arm across her shoulder and cradled her to him. She felt warm against him as they walked up to the bow of the ship and found a secluded spot to watch the ship depart from San Juan.

Within his embrace, Shauna stared at the glittering lights of the city, tiny golden jewels against a backdrop of black velvet. She sighed and nestled closer within his hold.

A few minutes later, she heard someone shout an order, then the stomping feet of the sailors as they scurried to their posts. The ship slid out of its berth and headed for open water. Without a word spoken, Shauna stood next to David and watched the shoreline fade from view. She felt the breeze wash over her, its salty tang clinging to her skin. David swung her around to face him. In the dark Shauna couldn't see David's face, but she could smell his masculine cologne and could feel his hot breath fan across her cheek. He bent his head closer. His lips joined hers in a hard, demanding kiss. Shauna's muscles became liquid as she melted against him. His kiss deepened until she thought she would faint. The blackness swirled before her eyes. Then suddenly he pulled away from her, his breathing short and raspy.

For a long moment Shauna felt his eyes drilling into her. She heard his breathing slow, but his fingers gripped her arms in a tight hold.

She bit her lower lip to still a cry and tore her arms from his ironclad hold. She moved back, unable to stand the silence that hung between them.

"Oh, Shauna, you're so refreshing! But I think for both our sakes we'd better call it a night." The words were whispered, but Shauna heard the masked passion that laced each word he spoke.

She stepped back further and murmured, "Yes, I think you're right." Her shaking hands grasped the railing until pain shot up her arms.

# Chapter Five

Shauna heard a pounding noise. She turned on her side and pulled the covers over her head. "Go away," she mumbled into her pillow, and tried to surrender to the world of sleep. But again that loud banging sound reached into the dark recesses of her mind and forced her to wake up.

She slipped out of bed, jerked her robe on, and padded to the door. "Who is it?" she asked, her face touching the cold metal of the door.

"It's Adam. Time to get up. I want to take you swimming on St. John today."

Shauna inched the door open and looked into the smiling face of Adam. She pushed her hair from her face and the bright light of the hallway accosted her eyes. Squinting, she said, "What time is it?"

"Eight o'clock and we just docked at the harbor of

St. Thomas. It's a beautiful day! Too beautiful to be sleeping, my friend. So rise and shine."

"Well, I don't know about shining, but I have risen." Shauna offered Adam a faint smile. "Can you give me fifteen minutes to get dressed?"

His smile widened. "Sure. I'll meet you up on the Main Deck in fifteen minutes by the place where we disembark."

Shauna nodded and closed the door. Walking into the bathroom, she splashed some cold water onto her face and whispered, "Fifteen minutes." She exhaled a breath of air slowly and began to wash her face and brush her teeth.

When she was selecting what shorts to wear, another knock sounded at the door.

"Yes," she said through the door.

"It's Mario. I have some flowers for you, Miss Peters."

Shauna opened the door and gazed into a bouquet of white roses. She sucked in her breath. Her eyes widened as she took in the two dozen roses in a white ceramic vase.

She buried her face in the flowers and smelled their sweet fragrance. "Oh, thank you, Mario. They are beautiful."

"Miss Peters, they are no more beautiful than you are. Some man must love you." The steward's eyes twinkled as he turned and made his way down the corridor toward the small kitchen near the stairs.

As she placed the vase on her nightstand and stared at them, the scent of the roses drifted toward her. A card stuck in them seemed to leap out at her. With trembling hands Shauna picked it out of the leaves and opened it. David Powell! She felt her skin tingle. "My favorite flower," she whispered.

Shauna placed the card by the vase and glanced at her watch. "Oh, no, only five more minutes." She scurried to her closet and pulled a red top and white shorts from their hangers. She quickly dressed and stuffed her swimming suit into a beach bag along with a towel, her suntan lotion, a hat, and her purse.

As she raced from her cabin and up the stairs to the Main Deck, she thought of David. I know so little about him. But an aura of power and authority surrounds him. He's exciting to be with . . . like Adam.

When she reached the lobby of the Main Deck, she scanned the milling crowd for Adam. He stood next to the elevator reading a pamphlet. Her gaze traveled over Adam, absorbing his handsome features—the firm mouth, the tanned skin, the black hair that curled on the nape of his neck, and his finely sculptured nose. She remembered the feel of those muscular arms around her, those sensual lips on hers. She shook her disturbing thoughts from her mind.

He's just a . . . friend, she repeated to herself.

Shauna strolled over to Adam and touched his arm. He jerked away as he looked at her. "Oh, it's you. I didn't hear you approach. Ready to go?"

"Yep. I've never snorkeled, so this should be fun."

"I hear the water at the National Park on St. John is beautiful."

They left the ship and Adam hailed a cab.

"We'd like to go to the harbor where we can get a boat to take us to St. John," Adam said to the driver as he slid into the back seat of the taxi.

As the cab pulled out onto the road and began its

climb up the hills of St. Thomas, Shauna was mesmerized by the beautiful scenery that sped by. She saw vivid flowers sprinkle the hillside, but what caught her breath was the sparkling water that glittered like diamonds. From the top of a hill the water looked almost silver as the sun's rays struck it.

When the cab halted at the small harbor on the other side of St. Thomas, Shauna was dazzled by the island. "I could live here forever, Adam, and be content to just lie in the sun and read all day long."

"Maybe for a week. But if I read you right, you'd become bored by the end of that week. You'd never be one to just sit around and do nothing. You're too intelligent not to use your talents in some way."

"Why, Adam, thank you."

They climbed out of the taxi and walked to the dock.

Adam approached a man on the dock and said, "I made reservations for a boat to take myself and another person to St. John for the morning. I'm Adam Steele."

"Ah, yes, Mr. Steele, I've been waiting for you. Come this way. We can leave immediately."

Shauna and Adam followed the man to a boat tied to the end of the pier. When they were seated, the captain untied the ropes that held the boat to the dock and started the engines. Shauna felt the motor roar into action.

She leaned back in the chair and let the breeze caress her. The sun wrapped her in its warmth. She closed her eyes and relived the previous evening. Again she won at the blackjack table. Again she felt David's lips crush hers in a demanding kiss. She rubbed her arms where she imagined the feel of his fingers boring into her flesh. She shuddered.

Shauna eased her eyes open when the boat slowed and maneuvered into a berth at the dock on St. John. She noticed that a taxi stood not three yards from the boat. Adam guided Shauna over to the driver.

"Can you take us to the National Park and wait for us?"

Shauna shot Adam a look. She whispered, "Adam, I will pay for this. It has to be expensive."

She winced when she saw Adam's eyes cloud with anger for a moment before, in a calm, controlled voice, he said, "When I ask someone on a date, I don't expect her to pay half, regardless of the cost. If I couldn't afford it, I wouldn't have planned this outing. I've saved all year for this trip and I want everything to be perfect. Don't mar it for me, Shauna."

She stepped back at the impact his harsh words had on her. "I didn't mean . . ." She gritted her teeth and slipped into the back seat of the cab.

In silence they covered the short distance to the National Park. Shauna caught glimpses of bays and hidden houses in the hills of St. John. I wish I owned one of those houses, she thought. This place is so peaceful.

As Shauna got out of the cab, she looked into Adam's face. A blank mask covered his features. She touched his arm and said, "I'm sorry for what I said back at the pier. Please, don't be mad at me," and flashed him a brilliant smile.

He gathered up the snorkeling equipment and took her elbow. "How can I stay mad at you for long? All you have to do is bat those big gray eyes at me and I'm all yours." His laugh rang in the sultry air.

They walked through the forest that edged the

shoreline to the beach. Shauna stared at the fine white sand that stretched to the sky-blue water, a blue so clear that she could see the coral reef from the shore.

Shauna threw her beach bag down and sat beside it on the sand. "Where do we change?"

Adam pointed toward a clump of trees. "Behind those trees."

She snapped her head around, eyes dilated. "I thought you told me there was a place to change into your swimming suit!"

He laughed, his roar echoing in the cove. "I did, didn't I?" He shrugged his shoulders and wiggled out of his shorts. He towered over her in his bathing suit, a broad grin plastered on his face. "Well, I suppose you have to take what you can get."

As Shauna stood, she noticed the devilish glint in his eyes and smiled. "Well, I hope I don't provide too much entertainment for the tourists." She trudged across the sand toward the trees. As she neared the edge of the beach, she saw a building nestled within the trees. Chuckling to herself, she headed for the structure.

She walked into the ladies' side of the building, quickly slipped out of her shorts and blouse, and donned her green two-piece swimsuit. By the time she had strolled back to the beach, Adam had the gear laid out on the sand.

"Ready for a quick lesson in how to use the equipment?" he asked, and handed her flippers, a face mask, and snorkel.

"There can't be much to it, Adam. I've worn a face mask and know what to do." Shauna spat on the plastic viewer and rolled the spit around until it covered the whole area. Then she leaned over and washed it in the water. After adjusting the straps to fit her head, she put the face mask on, then her flippers. "There. Now all I have to do is to put this end with the mouthpiece into my mouth and breathe normally." Shauna demonstrated and then started to wade out into the water.

When she was in the water up to her knees, she plunged the rest of her body into the salt water. She felt the cool water envelop her, easing the burning sensation of the sun. She stuck her face into the water and paddled out toward the coral reef. Suddenly something touched her leg. She jerked her head around and saw Adam swimming behind her. He waved. She turned back and concentrated on the multicolored fish that sped past her, scurrying to get out of her way. Stripes, bold yellows, and dull grays bombarded her eyes as schools of tiny fish darted away from her. Silence encased her in its peacefulness.

Shauna swam around the small island in the middle of the cove. As she headed back to the beach, she spied a large eel coming toward her. Panic swept through her as she thought of its deathly electric charge. She stared at the long, slick creature as it glided through the water nearer to her.

Oh, my God! Its teeth, she screamed silently. She thrashed about, salt water rushing into her snorkel. Jerking her head up, she yanked her face mask off and choked from the burning sensation in her throat. The eel passed within a foot of her but continued on its way out to sea.

Adam appeared next to her. "Are you all right?"

Coughs racked her body. She gasped, "No . . . swallowed . . . salt water." She grasped her neck and rubbed. Her lungs ached.

"Can you make it to shore?" Adam asked.

The concern was apparent in his voice. She nodded and swam next to him until they reached shallow water. Shauna stood, her legs trembling as she remembered the eel with its huge open mouth not one foot away from her.

Shauna stumbled and fell into the shallow water. Adam lifted her into his arms and carried her to their spread towels. He laid her down, then knelt beside her, smiling. "You had me worried for a moment. The best thing to do when you see something like an eel is to stay perfectly still. They won't bother you if you leave them alone."

"It was so ugly and menacing." Shauna tried to shake the image of the creature from her mind. "I think I've had enough snorkeling for today. It seems all I can do is drink the water." She again massaged her throat.

Adam extracted a thermos from his gear and poured Shauna a drink. "This is just fresh water, but it will help you." She gulped the cool liquid down and felt the searing pain in her throat ease.

Shauna lay down on the towel and closed her eyes. "I'm so tired." She turned over on her stomach and added, "Wake me when you are ready to go." Her body felt heavy as weariness took hold.

Shauna heard the surf as it pounded the beach. She heard voices in the distance and was drifting off to sleep when a hand shook her.

"I'm going to put some suntan lotion on you. I don't want you to burn." Adam massaged the cold liquid into her legs. As he rubbed her back with the lotion, a feeling of contentment wrapped her body. She rolled over and squinted, shielding her eyes from the sun's glare.

"You might as well finish the job." She shut her eyes and waited for him to apply the lotion to her front.

When his lips touched hers, she jerked open her eyes. She raised her hands to push him away but instead found herself enclosing him within her embrace as his kiss deepened. He smoothed damp strands of hair from her face and moved his lips in a soft trail from her mouth to her ear. He nibbled it and chills rose on her flesh as her blood turned to liquid fire and raced through her.

He pulled away and stared at her for a long moment, his eyes intense, his breath ragged. Silence fell between them as their gazes locked, searching each other.

He sat back on his heels and said, "I shouldn't have done that, but I'm not sorry, Shauna. I enjoyed it."

No words would form in her mind. She just stared at him until her eyes hurt from the glare of the sun. He moved to finish the job of rubbing suntan lotion on her when she finally said, "I enjoyed it, too."

He continued to apply the liquid without a word. When he was through, Shauna still felt the searing touch of his fingers on her flesh.

"Boy, is it hot today! I don't think I'll be able to stay out in the sun much longer." She fanned herself with her hat.

Without a backward glance, Adam stood and walked to the water. He waded out into the sea, then dove into the surf.

Shauna ran her finger across her lips and remembered the pressure of his mouth as it touched hers. She watched his arm lift out of the water and reach out in front of him in a long, graceful stroke. Shivering, she turned over onto her stomach and tried to concentrate on David Powell, but Adam's face lingered in her mind. David's what I want—a life of security, she told herself, but the excitement of Adam's kiss crept into her thoughts.

"So many places to shop, Adam!" Shauna looked down the long avenue of shops that lined the main street in Charlotte Amalie.

"Remember, the best buys are here on St. Thomas," Adam said as he guided Shauna into a jewelry shop.

Adam walked to the counter where the rings were displayed. Shauna followed. "Maybe I can help you with your selection."

He shot her a quick glance before saying to the salesgirl. "I would like to see your diamond rings."

The salesgirl nodded and extracted a tray of rings with huge diamonds in them. Shauna sucked in her breath.

"Your girl is mighty lucky, Adam. These rings are worth a fortune."

Adam fingered one ring with a large diamond in the middle and two smaller ones on the side of it. He held it up to the light. "Do you like this one, Shauna?"

"May I ask what the ring is for?"

"It will be her engagement ring." He turned the ring over and inspected it from all angles.

"If I were going to get an engagement ring, I would prefer an unusual one like that one." Shauna pointed through the glass to an emerald ring—one large stone in a setting of white gold.

Adam replaced the diamond ring and said, "Perhaps." He examined several more rings before shaking his head and saying, "I'm afraid you don't have what I want. Thank you."

As they walked away from the jewelry store, Shauna said, "You didn't tell me that you were engaged."

Adam shrugged. "Why? Would it have made any difference?"

"But . . ." Memory of the kiss that Adam had given her earlier that day seeped into her mind. Love. She laughed at the thought. Does it really exist? Or is there another emotion that we label love? Shauna felt the anger surge through her as she relived Mark's betrayal in that moment.

Adam stopped and turned to Shauna. "Would my being engaged make any difference to you?" He stared down at her, waiting.

For a moment Shauna's reply caught in her throat, but she tightened her jaw. "No," she answered finally, and walked past him.

But inside, Shauna seethed with rage. Men! How they use women! Well, this woman will do the using, she vowed silently.

# Chapter Six

Shauna gasped when she opened the door to her cabin and stared at a bouquet of yellow roses sitting next to her white ones. She walked to the nightstand and extracted the card.

Shauna, I hope you can meet me after dinner tonight for a drink.

Yours, David

Shauna's hands trembled. He's interested, she thought, and placed the card on top of the other one.

Pin pricks rose on her flesh as she sank onto her bunk and gazed at the bouquets. "Definitely interested," she whispered, "but I must make him more than just interested and soon, or in a few days he will leave for Chicago and I'll never see him again."

Shauna looked at herself in the mirror. "What can I wear tonight that will make him forget all the other women he has known in the past?"

In her mind Shauna searched her wardrobe for the perfect dress to wear. A long black gown high in the front but backless leaped into her thoughts. "That's it," she said aloud, and jumped to her feet. She moved to her closet and took the black dress from its hanger. Pulling a pair of black hose from her top drawer she thought, And this will be just the right touch with that slit up the back of the gown.

Shauna smiled and began to get ready for the evening. Thoughts of Adam teased her mind as she dressed, but she quickly banished them and replaced the picture of Adam with that of David, tall, powerfully built in a black tuxedo.

Shauna dabbed perfume at her wrists, then gathered up her black, beaded purse and left the cabin. Exultation threatened to overpower her as she walked toward the dining room. She entered and scanned the room for David. His seat at the captain's table was empty. A frown played at the corners of her mouth as she strolled to her table. Maybe business will keep him occupied through dinner and afterward, she thought, her frown deepening.

She stared at David's vacant seat until Adam's voice disturbed her. "So your friend isn't here tonight. Disappointed?"

Shauna swung her gaze to Adam as he sat next to her. She bit back a retort and gave him a tight smile. "It's none of your business," she finally whispered through clenched teeth.

He tossed back his head and laughed. "Now what have I done to deserve this?"

She glared at him. "If you must know, Adam Steele, I don't think your behavior is above reproach. What would your fiancée say if she knew about that kiss you gave me today?"

"And are you going to tell her?" His question mocked her.

She felt the harshness of his words and winced. "No, but I feel sorry for her. Men think it is fair to play around before and after marriage, but if a woman should, heaven forbid." Shauna lifted her chin, her eyes narrowed. "Always a double standard."

She turned her attention away from Adam and stared at her menu. The words fused together before her eyes as she tried to concentrate on what to eat. A lump formed in her throat and tears of frustration threatened to overcome her. She fought to control her emotions, but they welled within her. The walls seemed to close in on her. She leaped to her feet and fled the stuffy dining room. Halting only when she reached the railing at the back of the ship, she felt the breeze brush at her as the tears filled her eyes. Why do I let that man bother me so? she asked herself. He isn't what I want. He's engaged, poor, arrogant . . .

"Shauna, what's wrong?" Two strong arms drew her against a muscular chest. She leaned back and went limp within Adam's embrace.

Tears spilled onto her cheeks. She dashed them away and said, "Nothing. I guess I'm just tired, Adam."

Adam turned her around within the circle of his arms and tilted her chin up. His blue eyes darkened. Another tear formed on her eyelashes and dropped onto his shirt. He brushed the damp trail of tears away with a finger, then stroked the crease of sadness on her forehead, trying to smooth it away.

His soft voice cascaded over her as he whispered, "Don't cry, Shauna."

He bent and kissed the tip of her nose, then each eyelid. When his mouth claimed hers, she felt a tingling sensation spread through her. She willingly drowned herself in the passion he was drawing from her. Abruptly she twisted her head away and jerked back.

"No! Leave me alone! I don't want your kisses!" She hammered at his chest until her blows weakened and she fell against him, her face next to the soft material of his shirt.

"I want you, Shauna, but you're not ready. You don't know what you want in life." He pushed her away from him, then pivoted and walked from her.

Shauna watched his retreating figure. She leaned against the railing and held on to the wood for support as her legs buckled. Her grip on the railing tightened involuntarily until the strength returned to them. She straightened to her full height and said, "But I do know what I want. Money. Security." But those words sounded hollow to Shauna.

She swung around and faced the ocean. Security *is* what I want, she repeated to herself. Nancy *is* right.

Moments slipped by as Shauna watched the sun set, the rosy hue of the sky turning into dark blue. Adam's eyes when he looked at me a moment ago, she thought.

The sound of approaching footsteps caught Shauna's attention and held it. She glanced in the direction of the sound and saw David walking toward her. He smiled as she turned and gave him a broad smile. A picture of Adam when he walked away crept into her thoughts. No, she screamed silently, and focused her attention on David as he moved to stand next to her.

"Your friend told me I could find you out here." His gaze wandered the length of her, then returned to her face. "You look ravishing tonight."

Shauna heard the words that came so easily to his lips and saw his eyes that seemed so bright.

Shauna stared again at the sea. "He isn't a friend of mine. I just met him a few days ago."

"I just met you a few days ago and I hope that I'm more than a friend to you." David leaned closer to her.

Shauna felt his breath brush across her neck as his mouth caressed her neck, then moved to her ear. He kissed her lightly, then spun her around to face him. Crushing her to him, he kissed her again, but this time his mouth pressed into hers. She felt drained—an empty feeling replacing the swirling emotions of a moment ago.

David stepped back and stared at her. "I'm sorry. Obviously something is bothering you. Maybe I should leave you to your own thoughts." He turned to leave.

Shauna touched his arm. "Don't go," she whispered. "Please forgive me, but I have had a very tiring day." A faint smile spread across her face. "I'd like your company and the drink you promised me."

He held out his arm and said, "Then, in that case, let's go."

As they walked to the grand salon, Shauna said, "I must thank you for the beautiful flowers that you sent me. Roses are my favorite flower."

"I'm glad you liked them. Just my way of saying that I had a wonderful time last night." David glanced down at her and smiled.

He pulled out a chair for Shauna and she eased herself onto the cushion. From behind her she heard him order two drinks, then he sat next to her.

"Shauna, I'm having a little party tomorrow night and would like you to come."

She looked into his face and said, "I would love to. When?"

"At nine." David touched her hand, which was resting on the table.

She watched as one of his fingers ran down the length of her hand, brushing the flesh in a caress.

"I believe I'm going to enjoy getting to know you better, Shauna Peters."

Shauna felt the color rise in her cheeks. Her fingernails dug into the palm of her other hand, which lay in her lap. She shivered at his too-wide smile as an inner voice whispered, *Leave before it is too late. He doesn't play games and lose.*

Shauna patted her cheeks and nose with her powder puff, then applied some red lipstick. She turned and looked at the door when she heard a knock.

"Just a minute." Slipping on her robe, she walked to the door. When she opened it, she gasped. The steward held a large bouquet of red roses.

"You certainly have an admirer, ma'am." Mario handed her the flowers.

Words caught in her throat. She stared at the beautiful bouquet and swallowed hard. The man cleared his throat. She looked up at him and smiled. "Oh, thank you," she said, and took the vase.

Mario pivoted and began to move away. She inspected the bouquet, then called out to the steward, "There is no card with them. Who are they from?"

He turned and shrugged. "That's the way the roses came to my station. Sorry I can't help you." He flashed her a smile, then walked away.

Shauna watched the steward disappear into a room. She glanced at the roses, her mind racing with the possibilities of who sent them. It has to be David again, she thought, and closed her door. She placed the vase on her dresser and stepped back to admire the flowers. She counted twenty-four red roses and sucked in her breath. "A fortune. David must really be interested in me," she whispered.

Shauna slid her robe from her shoulders and down her arms. It fell to the floor in a pile about her feet, and she stepped over it as she walked to the closet. She withdrew a kelly green pantsuit of satinlike material and began to dress. Excitement took hold of her as the thought of the party in David's cabin grew within her, making her blood race through her veins.

One last time, she inspected herself in the mirror and smiled. She smoothed the material and turned around slowly. The green gleamed, catching the lights of the room. "Well, here goes," she whispered, and left her cabin.

As she neared David's suite, her mouth went dry and a knot formed in her throat. She ran her tongue over her lips and sucked in gulps of air. Clenching her purse tighter, she knocked on the door.

David opened it, his face lit with a wide grin. "Good

evening, Shauna." His gaze flickered over her before he stepped aside and waved her into the room.

She walked into the middle of the living area and spun around. Her eyes grew wide. "Where is everyone? I'm not too early, am I?"

He laughed. "No, Shauna. You're the only guest I invited to the party. Why have boring people standing around talking too much when you and I can be alone to enjoy each other?"

Shauna felt the knot in her throat tighten. She swallowed hard, then turned to survey the suite. Noticing that the door to the bedroom was slightly ajar, she quickly diverted her gaze from it and took in the two soft-looking sofas facing each other with a coffee table between them, a table with a tray of hors d'oeuvres, and a bucket with a bottle of champagne in it. Facing David, she felt at a loss for words and her mind refused to function.

David strode across the room and slipped her shawl from her shoulders. He massaged her upper arms and whispered into her ear, "Relax. I won't bite. I much prefer your company than a group of people, all vying to please or impress me."

Shauna felt her muscles tense. She stepped away from David and fingered the back cushion of the sofa. "You don't care much for people, do you?"

His laughter echoed through the cabin. "Only when they can serve my purpose. I'm much too busy to take the time for small talk or for people that can't help me."

"And how am I to help you, David?"

"I get such pleasure from just looking at you." He touched her arm and drew her back against him.

"Shauna, you'll learn soon enough to be the user, not the person used. It's so much better."

She twisted around and looked him in the eye. "Am I to be used by you?"

He lowered his gaze, his eyes half closed. "No—I'm talking about business, my dear," came his quiet reply.

"Oh, I see." She forced a gay tone into her voice. "That certainly makes a difference. But I'll remember what you said if I ever do business with you."

He shook his head. "My, how did we ever get into such a serious conversation? I planned this evening to be entertaining, amusing, not heavy with my philosophy of life."

She watched him walk to the table and remove the champagne bottle from the silver bucket. He inched the cork from the bottle and poured two glasses of the sparkling liquid. After handing one glass to Shauna, he held his up to toast her. "To the most beautiful woman on board."

Shauna smiled, then sipped her champagne. The bubbles tickled her nose. She rubbed it then took another swallow of her drink. She began to relax as she finished the first glass of champagne and held it out for David to refill it.

"Have a seat. I'll put some music on."

Shauna's gaze followed David's movements as he flipped through a stack of records and chose one. He placed it on the stereo, then came to sit beside her on the sofa. She felt his flesh touch hers. Her skin tingled and she quickly gulped the champagne down in three swallows.

David arched one brow. "More?"

Shauna nodded and gave him her glass. She kicked off her shoes. I feel so much better. She sighed at the thought.

He glanced over his shoulder and asked, "Do you want anything to eat? I have a tray of food here that the chef made especially for me."

"Not now. Maybe later." Shauna felt the muscles in her stomach begin to loosen.

I must eat, she told herself. It isn't good to drink on an empty stomach. The thought slipped into her mind for a brief second before she pushed it away. A protecting warmth enveloped her. I'm here with a handsome, wealthy man. Alone with him. And he's interested in me. Perhaps in love with me. Her mind reeled with the possibility of becoming David's wife. I am beautiful, he says. I am intelligent. I would make him a good wife.

But the wild, fiery sensations that Adam evoked in her intruded into her thoughts. She heard those words again. *I want you, Shauna, but you're not ready. You don't know what you want in life.*

Oh, yes, I do, she thought. I don't want to be hurt again.

David eased down next to her and placed her glass on the coffee table. His arm slid around the back of the sofa and his hand rested on her shoulder. She looked up at him and smiled. Yes, a good wife.

The silence stretched between them as his gaze touched hers and held it in his power. One minute became two. Her breath caught in her lungs as he bent and kissed her, and their lips joined softly. Shauna heard the music in the background float across the room and envelop her in its caress. She was on fire as his kiss deepened and he pulled her against him. The muscles of his arms grew taut, rock hard as he clasped her to him.

Something clicked within her mind. She brought her hands up between them and pushed David from her. For a brief second Shauna saw anger flash in his eyes before he masked the emotion with a questioning look.

Shauna leaned over and grasped the stem of the glass. She took several swallows and gripped the glass tighter to keep her hand from shaking. When he moved closer, she rose, slid her feet into her shoes, then walked to the porthole. Gazing out at the midnight blue water, she thought the sky appeared a shade lighter with a large full moon touching the horizon.

"What a beautiful view you have. I don't have a porthole in my cabin. Of course, I'm rarely there, so I don't miss much." Words tumbled from her lips, her nerves stretched tight.

"You are welcome to come look out my porthole any time you want. In fact, the sunrise is beautiful to watch from this window."

He stood and crossed the room. Shauna could feel his breath touch her neck and smelled his cologne. She shivered and rubbed her upper arms to warm her chilled body. "I didn't think a man like you would be up that early."

He laughed. "A man like me? What kind of man do you think I am, Shauna?"

She ran her fingers around the rim of the porthole as he touched her hair, brushing it away from her cheeks. "One who doesn't need to get up at the crack of dawn. Someone who delegates power and duty to others while he enjoys himself. Someone who doesn't have to work himself to death to stay even."

His hands wrapped around her upper arm. He whispered, "Shauna, I work hard because I love to work, to make things happen. I enjoy the power I have. If I delegate too much work to others, I lose some of that power. I don't want that."

He kissed her neck. She felt weak as she sagged against him. He turned her around within his embrace and claimed her mouth in a hard kiss that drew the rest of the strength from her.

She half floated, half walked back to the sofa.

"When I saw you that night looking at me, I knew we would become good friends." His whispered words permeated her dazed mind. She heard the husky voice as he continued to whisper endearments to her, but it sounded so far away.

With kiss after kiss he eased Shauna back onto the sofa until his body covered hers. His hands roamed down the length of her body, then rested upon a breast.

Alarm penetrated her senses. "No, David!"

He stifled her protest with another kiss, his mouth bruising, pressing. She tore her lips from his and whipped her head from side to side shouting, "No!"

His grip tightened around her arms. She froze as panic seized her and squeezed the breath from her.

Remain calm, she said to herself. This isn't right. I must get out of here. She fought to control her rapidly beating heart, her constricting throat.

Inhaling a deep breath, she shoved David from her with all her strength and scrambled to her feet, panting. For a brief second he remained motionless, a surprised expression etched into his features.

"Why you . . ." he muttered, and stood.

His face was like thunder, his eyes lightning. She backed away, her body pressing into the door. He took several steps toward her and thrust his face within inches of hers.

"You led me on. You teased me and now play the innocent virgin. You women are all alike. Playing games. Either you're cold or so eager to fall in bed that you trip over your own two feet."

With breasts heaving, Shauna narrowed her eyes and glared at David. Her anger surfaced as she said through clenched teeth, "Men!" She clutched her hands to her chest and took another breath. "I never led you on. That's what you wanted to read in my actions. I thought there was more between us."

"That's what you wanted to read, Shauna." He laughed, a hideous sound that reverberated throughout the room. "Marriage! Never! I don't want to be tied to one woman. No fun." His laughter increased.

Shauna half turned and placed her hand on the doorknob.

His hideous laugh still echoed throughout the cabin. "You know you don't want to leave."

She straightened. "I don't want to ever see you again."

"Shauna, you're a very desirable woman. Quit playing hard to get."

The breath in her lungs felt trapped and her throat closed. He pulled her to him.

A noise. A knock at the door disturbed the tension-filled air. Shauna twisted her head around to look at the door as the pounding penetrated the stillness again.

"Shauna Peters, I must see you immediately. It's urgent."

Shauna sighed. Adam, she thought, then aloud she said, "I suggest you answer your door, Mr. Powell."

David cursed and strode to the door. He jerked it open and stepped aside to admit Adam. Adam surveyed the cabin before his gaze rested upon Shauna. He looked down the length of her, then walked over to her and took her hand. He led her from the cabin. Shauna collapsed into Adam's arms as the door slammed shut behind them.

"Oh, Adam, I've never been so glad to see your face." She trembled with relief.

"Come on, Shauna. Let's get away from here." Adam fitted her into the crook of his arm and led her down the corridor.

Shauna relived David's "party for two." She again heard his hideous laughter, which seemed to fill her whole mind.

Nancy, I wish I'd never allowed you to talk me into that plan of yours to end all my worries. I think I have more problems now than when I came aboard this ship, Shauna said to herself.

"Are you all right, Shauna?" Adam's voice sounded so husky, deep.

She nodded. "I think so." Shauna looked around for the first time at her surroundings. "Where am I?"

"My cabin. You look so pale and my cabin is just one deck below David Powell's." He shrugged. "So I brought you here."

"Thank you, Adam," Shauna whispered, a lump forming in her throat. "I don't know what I would have done if you hadn't come along." Shauna reached out and ran her fingers along Adam's jawline. She offered him a smile.

Slowly, Adam inclined his head and said, "You are welcome, my dear. I'm available anytime for the service of rescuing a fair damsel in distress."

Shauna laughed. "And how, kind sir, were you so lucky to be in the right place at the right time?"

"Would you believe I just happened to be walking by and heard your sweet voice?"

Shauna shook her head.

"Well, then how about that I know what kind of man David Powell is and was lurking around the dark corridors of this ship waiting for any sign that you might need rescuing? Some knights just have to go out and drum up business."

"Can't you be serious, Adam Steele?"

"Oh, but I am serious. The company I work for does business with David Powell's. I have heard some nasty rumors about him."

Shauna felt the color drain from her face. "Rumors? What kind?"

Adam raised both eyebrows and said, "I'll never tell. I won't be accused of gossiping."

"You don't have to tell me. I can imagine what the rumors were. X-rated, no doubt, if I know our Mr. Powell." A shudder ran through her body and she wrapped her arms around herself.

Adam gathered Shauna into his arms and whispered into her ear, "I'm here. You have nothing to worry about."

Shauna laid her head on Adam's shoulder. "I don't

want to ever see that man again." Another tremor bolted through her body as her eyes misted. "What if I do see him again? What will I do without you there?" Tears rolled down her cheeks and fell on his shirt.

"Shh. You won't. He will stay away from you." Adam tightened his hold on her. He patted Shauna's back and rocked gently with her in his arms. "Cry, Shauna. You'll feel better afterward."

The tears flowed. The feeling of failing again over-whelmed Shauna. Between her sobs she mumbled, "Nothing works. I've been a fool."

"Don't be so hard on yourself. How were you to know what kind of man David Powell is behind that mask he wears? Many women have fallen for his line and not fared as well as you did. If I have anything to say about it, Mr. Powell won't get near you again."

Shauna heard Adam's angry words. She pulled away and wiped the tears from her cheeks. Sniffling, she said, "Never again will I be blind to a man because of his money. I was wrong. *Nancy* was wrong."

Adam arched an eyebrow. "Nancy?"

Shauna leaned back against the wall and stretched her legs out on the bunk. "Nancy is my best friend. She was the one who convinced me that I'd be better off marrying someone rich. No more worries, no more cares."

A puzzled expression washed over Adam's face. "You don't seem like a lady who can be talked into something she doesn't want herself."

Shauna wrung her hands together in her lap. "I suppose normally not, but I believe I was still in a state of shock. My fiancé married a friend of mine and wrote me a letter afterward to let me know." Shauna looked Adam in the eye. "He didn't even have the decency to tell me in person. The letter was delivered to the courthouse after my first big victory."

Adam's face darkened. "Men like your fiancé and David Powell are not worth a second thought from you."

"But Mark and I had been together for four years! How can you just write off four years of your life? I was hurt, humiliated. I thought Nancy was right. I was tired of working hard—and for what?" Shauna choked back more tears.

"To be a successful lawyer. To be your own person. Those things are important, Shauna. Very important. You don't need Mark, David, or money to be really happy. Happiness is within you, what you make out of your life. Don't depend on anyone else for it."

Shauna took Adam's hand and squeezed it. "I like you, Adam Steele. You are a nice man."

Adam cupped Shauna's chin in his hand and said, "And I like you, Shauna Peters. You are a nice woman."

The moment became suspended in time as Shauna looked into Adam's eyes and felt the magnetic force that emanated from him. He leaned closer to her, his lips brushing hers in a fleeting kiss.

Shauna turned her gaze away from Adam's and glanced around the cabin. "Your room isn't much bigger than mine."

"Room might be too kind of a word for this cabin. How about closet?"

Shauna's laughter filled the room. "Not a bad description." Shauna's gaze rested upon the travel clock by the bunk. "I think I'd better be going. It's late and I know you must be getting your beauty sleep."

"Yes. When you reach thirty that becomes a necessity."

"Well, thank goodness I have four more years to go."

Adam helped Shauna up. "They go quickly, Shauna. Enjoy each moment while it's here."

She stood on tiptoes and kissed Adam on the cheek. "I will."

Adam quickly turned and fumbled for his keys on the nightstand. "I'll walk with you to your cabin."

"That's not necessary. I'm fine."

"Just as a precaution, my dear. We don't want any more ugly scenes with David Powell."

She smiled. "Thanks."

In silence they walked through the darkened hallways to Shauna's cabin. When Shauna turned at her door to say good night, Adam took her key and opened the door. He stuck his head into the room, then stepped back. "The coast is clear. No one is sitting there waiting for you."

"He wouldn't, would he?"

"No, he wouldn't. I shouldn't have teased you so." He held her hand. "There's no reason for him to bother you anymore. I think you made your point tonight." He let her hand slip to her side. "Now you get a good night's sleep and I'll see you tomorrow morning at breakfast."

Nodding, she watched as he turned and walked down the corridor toward the stairs. She stared at his retreating figure until he disappeared around the corner, then spun around and made her way into her cabin. Searching through the dark shadows, she checked the bathroom before releasing her pent-up breath and lying back on the bed.

She stared at the ceiling, her mind reeling with her thoughts. Fool! I was so wrong. Never again will I listen to someone else. She scowled. David Powell should be locked away. A picture of Adam seeped into her thoughts. Thank heaven for Adam. What would I have done if it hadn't been for him? The image of Adam vanished as her eyes grew heavier and heavier. Sleep descended and whisked her into a dreamless world.

# Chapter Seven

Shauna slipped on her bathing suit cover and slid her feet into her sandals. She checked her purse for the suntan lotion and her key, then picked up a towel and started for the door. When she opened it, her eyes widened as they took in the person standing in the doorway. When she dropped the towel and her purse, the thud vibrated within the cabin.

"May I come in?" David asked, and pushed Shauna into the room. He shut the door behind him and turned to stare at her.

"Get out of here this instant! If you don't, I will scream until someone comes."

"I wouldn't do that if I were you. I told you once that I'm a rich and powerful man. I have my ways of making you regret embarrassing me in front of anyone. I hope you understand what I'm saying."

Her heartbeat raced in panic, the blood coursing

through her veins. She twisted her hands together and squeezed them tightly until they turned white.

"Please, just leave me alone," Shauna cried, and took several steps back into the center of the cabin.

David closed the gap between them with two strides and took Shauna's chin in his grasp. "You are so beautiful."

Those words made Shauna tremble. She bit her lip, her mind swirling with her thoughts. Humor this man. Get away from him before . . . Shauna swallowed hard and backed further away.

She backed into the nightstand and gripped the edge of the table, her fingernails digging into the wood. "What do you want, David? I am supposed to meet someone right now." The pressure in her chest increased until she thought she was going to suffocate.

He waved his hand in the air and laughed. "Oh, nothing much. I just wanted to return your shawl. I thought it might help to keep you warm when you get cold at night." His grin became a sneer as he hurled the shawl at her.

She caught it and tossed it on the bunk. "I have my shawl now. Thank you." She stepped to one side and tried to move past him. "Now I really must be going."

He reached out and grabbed her arm. "Not yet. Aren't you going to thank me better than that?"

"No!" she spat.

He covered her mouth with his and drew her to him. His fingers bit into the flesh of her upper arms. She twisted from his grip and fled from the cabin.

His laughter followed her as she ran down the corridor. The hideous sound faded as her footsteps pounded up the stairs. After racing up three flights of stairs, Shauna halted and glanced over her shoulder. She saw only an elderly couple gawking at her from the bottom step. Half smiling, she began to walk through the grand salon toward the pool. She gazed down at her shaking hands and clenched them into fists. "Stay calm," she whispered, but she still trembled from the memory of his kiss, the look of lust deep within David's eyes.

When she stepped outside into the sunlight, she squinted and searched the deck chairs for Adam. Please be here, she prayed silently. She made her way among the chairs until she gazed down at him, lounging in the sun.

Adam looked up at her. His face creased with a frown. "You look like you have just seen a ghost. What happened?" He moved over and pulled Shauna down to sit next to him on the deck chair.

Words refused to form on her lips. She just stared at Adam with her body tense, her hands balled in her lap.

"It was David, wasn't it?"

She nodded.

"Shauna," Adam said as his frown deepened. "What did he do? He didn't . . ."

Shauna moved her head from side to side. In a raspy voice she whispered, "No. He came to return my shawl, but . . ."

Adam's eyes turned a dark blue, like the ocean during a storm. "I think I'd better have a word with that man now!"

Adam started to rise, but Shauna restrained him with a hand. She could hear the fear creep into her voice as she spoke. "No. Adam, he's too powerful. He'd destroy you if you stood in his way. He's cruel. He doesn't care what he does to people. I don't want to have your job on my conscience. Please, Adam, let's forget the whole incident."

She watched Adam's eyes become slits. He stared across the pool and the silence became unbearable as Shauna chewed on her bottom lip, waiting for his answer.

"Please, don't make things worse," she said.

Adam eased back down onto the deck chair and took Shauna's hands within his. "I wouldn't want to do anything to upset you, but that man should be taught a lesson."

"And I agree. Someday someone will, but we aren't in a position of power to do it."

Adam lowered his gaze. "Maybe not," he muttered, letting Shauna's hands fall from his grasp.

She lay down in her deck chair and stretched out. "Do you have some suntan lotion and a towel? I left my cabin in rather a hurry and have no intention of returning for quite a while."

"Then I'll get them for you. Stay here and don't leave."

"Adam, don't go. I don't need them. I'll just use your towel and I think my tan is dark enough to stay out here for an hour."

Adam threw her a glance over his shoulder. "Don't worry. David Powell won't wait around for you to return. I won't be long." He strode toward the doors that led to the grand salon.

Shauna's gaze followed his movements until he disappeared. She blew her pent-up breath out through pursed lips and leaned back against the deck chair.

What a mess I have made of things, she chided herself. But again Adam has made me feel safe, protected. She closed her eyes and relished the feel of the warm sun as it bathed her in its golden rays. Adam Steele—a strong name, a strong man. The name lingered in her mind as she drifted off to sleep. . . .

A man with blond hair and black eyes stared down at Shauna before descending on top of her. His massive hand stifled her screams as they tore from her throat. She felt her eyes water and the man was seen through a haze of tears as he ripped at her clothes. A hideous sound exploded from his lips. Shauna lashed out at the man that covered her with his hard strength. She pummeled his back and tried to bite his hand. He brought his hand back and slapped her across the cheek. She felt fire spread through her as he struck her over and over. A moan welled up from her throat and was expelled in anguish. Pain. Pawing hands. Foul breath.

Shauna bolted upright in her deck chair. Her eyes widened. Ramrod straight, she surveyed the tranquil scene before her and relaxed, the tension of her nightmare slipping away.

She watched Adam walk across the deck toward her, his face set in grim lines. He approached her with a bottle of suntan lotion in his hand and a towel slung over his arm.

"Sorry I'm late, but it took me awhile to find the things you wanted."

"They were right there on the floor." She took the bottle and towel. "Probably David Powell took great pleasure in hiding them from me." Shauna's jaw quivered with rage. "I hope I have seen the last of him. Next time he won't catch me off guard. He'll rue the day he tries to bother me again." Her courage grew from the flames of fear and hate. She unscrewed the cap on the bottle and started to apply the lotion to her legs. With vicious strokes she rubbed the clear liquid into her skin until it gleamed.

"If David Powell is smart, he won't stay on the ship when we land in Montego Bay."

Shauna cocked her head to one side and raised one eyebrow. "Oh? No, Adam, he isn't a man that runs from trouble. He relishes it, for it makes him feel powerful."

"Powerful men have their vulnerable points as we all do," Adam said, and closed his eyes.

Shauna lay back on the deck chair and listened to the sounds of the ship as it glided through the calm waters of the Caribbean. The sound of the waves as they lapped at the sides of the ship penetrated her thoughts. She focused on that noise and blocked from her mind the chattering of the people around her. She was alone, floating across the sea. But to where? she asked herself. She felt a hollow feeling gnaw at her.

A hand shook her arm. She opened her eyes halfway and gazed at Adam's face. "You'd better turn over or you will burn." He pressed his finger into the skin on her forearm. The indentation turned white, enclosed by reddened flesh.

"I think I've lain in the sun long enough today. I believe I'll rest before lunch."

"Then I'll escort you back to your cabin and check everything out for you."

"You don't . . ."

He placed his hand over her mouth. "No protests. I won't listen. You would be wasting your breath."

Shauna gathered her belongings and made her way with Adam to her cabin.

When Adam and Shauna entered the cabin, Shauna stood by the door while Adam inspected the small room and bathroom. "No sign of David Powell."

Shauna grinned. "I really didn't think he would be lurking in the shower stall. Not his style."

A grin appeared on Adam's face. "Don't think so, but you can never tell about a man like that." He walked to the door and opened it. "See you at lunch. I'll escort you to the dining room. Pick you up at eleven-fifty."

"I feel like a witness for the state, having to be guarded twenty-four hours a day."

"Maybe not twenty-four hours, but I'd feel better knowing you are safe from him," Adam said, and stepped out into the hallway. He flashed her a brilliant smile before closing the door.

She listened to his retreating footsteps before she walked into the bathroom and started her shower. A warm spray of water pounded at her flesh, refreshing her. She stood motionless and let the water hit her with its force as droplets cascaded over her. Moments passed with her attention riveted to the warm feeling encasing her, making her relax for the first time in a while. She tuned out everything except the feel of the water and the sound of it splashing against the wall.

Finally she shut the water off, stuck her arm out of the shower stall, and found a towel. After drying off, she searched for her robe and slipped it on before stepping out into the cold room. A sudden knock disturbed the quiet of the cabin.

"Who is it?"

"Mario, ma'am."

Shauna sighed and opened the door. The steward stood grinning from ear to ear, holding a single perfect yellow rose.

Shauna shook her head. "I don't want it. Take it away."

"But, Miss Peters, what am I to do with it? It's so beautiful."

"Throw it in the sea. I don't care." She slammed the door shut and collapsed against the wood. Leave me alone, David Powell. What are you trying to do to me? she screamed within her mind.

Shauna smashed her hand into the wood of the door. "I won't let him bother me or ruin my vacation," she whispered, but shook with mounting rage.

"I'll stick," Shauna said.

She watched the dealer flip a nine over and the player next to her cursed as he busted.

"The dealer pays nineteen, twenty, and twenty-one." The man stacked five white chips in front of Shauna.

· She twisted around and exclaimed to Adam, "I won again. But I doubt I would have without your advice. Where did you learn to play blackjack so well?"

"I've been to Las Vegas once or twice in my time."

"This is exciting. I've made fifty dollars in less than half an hour."

"Another lesson you should learn is to quit while you're ahead."

"Okay. I'll play one more round and then give up my chair. It's getting stuffy in here and I think it would be nice to go for a walk around the ship. Care to join me in a stroll?"

Shauna watched as she was dealt a four and a ten and feeling daring, took another card. When the dealer gave her a six, she smiled, and waited to see what the dealer would do. When he turned a queen and a seven over, she gasped with excitement. The dealer handed her three red chips. She gathered up the rest of her winnings and walked to the cashier, a smile plastered on her face.

"Seventy dollars! I still can't believe it! First in San Juan and now here. I've never gambled before in my life. Money was so hard to come by I couldn't spare it if I wanted to. I might just quit being a lawyer and become a gambler."

Adam threw her a searching look. "It's not something I would make a habit of. But you should go to the racetrack in New Orleans and enjoy a day there. It's fun to cheer your horse to victory."

"I just might do that when I get home." They walked along the back of the ship and stopped to gaze out at the dark sea. "I'll hate to see this cruise come to an end in two days." She turned to face Adam. "This has certainly been a trip to remember."

"Yes, but we both have to go back to our lives in Dallas and New Orleans. You have your work and I have my . . ."

Shauna stared into Adam's blue eyes. "And you have

your fiancée. I had almost forgotten about her. Why didn't she come with you on the trip? She has great faith in you to let you come on this cruise by yourself."

"Shauna, I make my own decisions. I needed a week by myself without any interruptions before I go back to Dallas and carry on with my life. I just left without telling anyone where I was going."

"Why?"

"I had things to sort out. Marriage is a big step for me. If I take it, it will be a permanent step. I don't believe in divorce."

Shauna lowered her gaze and studied the sea. Rolling waves splashed against the hull of the ship.

"What's she like?"

"Beautiful, delicate as a rose, fragile as a piece of china—everything a man would want in a wife. A perfect hostess, always dressed just right. She doesn't argue but instead rationally talks things out with you."

"Sounds boring to me," Shauna muttered.

"What did you say?"

Shauna swung her gaze to meet Adam's. "Oh, nothing." They looked at each other for a long moment before Shauna broke the silence by saying, "Isn't the moon beautiful? I love to see a full moon on a clear night when all the stars are twinkling against the dark backdrop of the sky." Shauna breathed deeply. "And the air is heavy with the scent of the sea."

"It's hard to find a more romantic place," Adam whispered as he leaned against the railing. "I love the ocean. The air is so clean, not like in the cities where smog hangs heavy."

"I know. The air in New Orleans is bad."

His arm slid around her shoulder and she nestled

within his embrace as she stared out across the water. The minutes slipped by with Shauna only hearing the sounds of the sea and the distant music.

"I suppose all wonderful evenings must come to a close. It's getting late and we dock at Montego Bay early tomorrow morning," Shauna said.

"Will you accompany me on a tour of the city and the hilly countryside?"

She nodded. "I'd love it!"

"Good, then we'll leave after breakfast."

The fields of banana trees sped by as the taxi she and Adam were in headed for the town. She turned her head around and saw the ship anchored in the bay and motorboats full of passengers going to and from the ship.

"The last launch leaves the harbor at four-forty-five," she said.

"We'll probably be back at the ship before then."

"Good. I would hate to miss the boat and have to stand on the dock watching the ship sail away."

As the taxi drove down the main street, Shauna noticed a policeman standing in a box in the middle of an intersection directing the traffic. They passed him and headed toward the marketplace.

When the cab halted by the row of stalls in the marketplace, Adam leaned forward and asked, "Can you wait for us? We would like to do some shopping but shouldn't be gone too long."

"Must pay," the cab driver grumbled.

"I will. After the marketplace I would like to drive into the hills and then along the coast."

The driver nodded and turned to face straight ahead.

Shauna shrugged and climbed out of the taxi. After walking a few paces from the cab, she mumbled to Adam, "He's certainly a friendly person."

Adam smiled. "At least he agreed to wait for us. Probably will charge us an arm and a leg for it though."

Shauna stopped and pulled on Adam's arm. He halted. "Adam, let me pay half of the taxi. It's only fair that I do. You work hard for your money just like I do."

He arched an eyebrow. "How do you know I work hard for my money?"

"Well . . . well, just knowing you makes me feel that way." She felt the blush spread over her face.

His smile widened. "You're right. I do work hard and value the money I earn. You can pay half if you want."

"Good. Now let's go into that first stall. I want to look at those straw bags. Just perfect for the beach."

"Remember to haggle over the price. They love to do that here."

Shauna removed her sunglasses and searched through a mountain of straw bags before finding the one she wanted. Turning to the girl at the counter, she asked, "How much?"

"Five American dollars."

"I'll give you three for it."

The girl shook her head and paused to think. "I'll accept four dollars. That's my final price."

A determined look came in the girl's eyes and Shauna thrust the bag into the girl's hand and said, "I'll take it." She followed the girl to the counter by the door and paid her.

When Shauna emerged from the stall, she squinted and fumbled through her purse for her sunglasses. She put them on and scanned the crowd. Adam stood across from her inspecting a rack of shirts.

"I like that one," Shauna said as she approached him.

He held the white and brown shirt and turned it around. "Not bad, but not me."

"The shirt would look great with jeans. Maybe not your ten-gallon hat and cowboy boots, but with jeans it would."

He put the shirt back on the rack and pivoted. "I don't wear jeans much. Ready to go?"

Shauna stared at Adam as he began to walk away. He turned and extended his hand for her. "Aren't you coming?"

"You don't wear jeans much! I thought everyone wore jeans all the time nowadays."

"Well, I guess I'm the exception to that rule. Never found the time to just lounge around in casual clothes. All that hard work we talked about. Remember?"

"Oh," was all Shauna could manage to say. She took Adam's hand and walked beside him to the taxi.

As she slipped into the back seat, she said, "I really don't know much about you, Mr. Steele."

He flipped his hand in the air. "There isn't much to tell. I work, I sleep, I eat, and I occasionally play."

"At what?"

"Tennis, reading, swimming, et cetera."

The driver slid behind the wheel and started the engine. Adam gave him some directions and the cab lurched forward. Shauna's head whipped back, then forward, before the car slipped into the correct gear and the driver maneuvered it into the main road.

She tilted her head to one side and slanted a look at Adam. "You know, I've been with you every day for almost a week and I still know next to nothing about you. What does 'et cetera' mean, Adam Steele?"

"Only boring things that everyone does with their everyday life."

"Well, you can at least tell me what you are going to wear to the masquerade ball tonight. I want to be able to pick you out from the crowd."

His laughter floated from his throat. "No way, Shauna. That's half the fun of it. You will have to guess what I am."

Shauna flipped her head around and stared out the window. "If that's the way you want it, I might not even try to find you tonight."

She felt Adam's hand brush the hair from her neck. "I'll make you a bet. I'll discover who you are before you find out who I am."

She twisted her head around to stare into Adam's face. "A bet?"

He nodded. "Is it a deal?"

"What are we betting?"

"If I win, you have to give me a kiss." He extended his hand out for her to shake. "And if you win I will buy you a gift."

She paused, looked at his hand, then took it and shook it. "A deal."

Adam leaned back against the seat and looked out his window. Shauna studied his features, his brows knitted, his mouth set in a neutral expression. What are you thinking, Adam Steele? she wondered. Is it the same thing as I am? I hope you win the bet tonight. She thought back to his earlier kisses and hungered for the feel of his mouth upon hers. Oh, why do you have to be engaged?

# Chapter Eight

Shauna smiled at her reflection in the mirror, taking in the tight black pants, the billowing white shirt, the knee-high black boots, and the bandanna covering her auburn hair. She started to pull out a few strands of her hair to curl on her neck, then halted. Not fair to give myself away, she thought. Besides, I don't need for Adam Steele to give me another kiss. I can't fall for a man in love with another woman.

She looked at herself again in the mirror and spoke to the image. "You have already been hurt once. Don't make the mistake of having it happen to you twice and in one month's time."

She picked up her mask and adjusted it on her face. "I'll just have to find him first and settle for that gift he promised me. Much safer." She turned away from the mirror and walked from the cabin.

When Shauna entered the ballroom of the grand salon, she scanned the crowd. Where is he? she wondered. There were George Washingtons, Napoleons, Caesars, Indians, but no one that looked like Adam Steele.

*Look for someone tall with a muscular build,* an inner voice said.

Maybe he isn't here yet, she thought and strolled about, nodding at a few people who spoke as she moved among the crowd of merrymakers.

Shauna saw a man with his back to her standing towering over a woman dressed in a Marie Antoinette outfit. His massive shoulders filled the costume he wore; his black hair gleamed in the lights. Shauna inched her way to him and tapped him on the shoulder. "I found you first. You have lost, Adam."

When the man turned around, Shauna saw his brown eyes through the slits of his mask.

"Adam? Who are you looking for? I'm with my wife, lady. I don't know you."

Shauna backed away saying, "I'm sorry. Wrong person." She looked from the man to the woman. The woman's hand was on her hip as she tapped her fan against her gown. Shauna pivoted and fled the couple, putting the room between them. Have to be more careful next time, she thought, and began to study the men around her.

For the next half an hour Shauna searched the ballroom for Adam. She finally collapsed into a chair as she found the same men parading in front of her. He's just not here yet, she told herself, and put her feet on a table in front of her. The tight boots pinched her toes and she longed to pull them off and wiggle her toes in the soft carpet of the salon. Instead she signaled a waitress and ordered a drink.

As she sipped her Imperial, two hands covered her eyes behind their massive flesh. "Guess who?"

Shauna slumped forward. "How did you find me, Adam? I have been looking for you and haven't seen anyone that looked like you at all. Well, except one man." His hand slipped away. Adam took two strides from behind the chair and towered over Shauna.

She brought her hand up to stifle her giggles. "A clown! You look ridiculous. Just look at that big red nose and white makeup! I can't believe it!"

Shauna stared at him as he bowed deeply, sweeping his arm across his body. "Adam Steele at your service, ma'am." Adam moved closer. "And now for my kiss."

Shauna saw the gleam appear in his blue eyes. She raised her hands and stopped him. "Oh, no, Adam Steele, not in that makeup. I don't care to have white all over my face. If you choose to, fine. But not me."

His face creased with a pout. "You aren't going to back out on your bet?"

"No, but I won't kiss you until you wash your face."

A smile slipped through his pouting lips as he bowed again and said, "I'll see what I can do to change that." He pivoted and walked away.

Shauna sipped her drink and waited for Adam to reappear, her fingers tapping the arm of the chair in time with the music. The band played seven songs before Adam strolled through the double doors and headed toward her. She noticed that he was now dressed casually, his eyes twinkling.

When he stood over Shauna, he took her hand and

drew her up out of the chair. He pulled her along behind him through the double doors out onto the deck. The wind blew the folds of Shauna's shirt and the length of scarf that trailed down her back. Shauna smelled the air, heavy with the scent of rain. She scanned the gray sky above and saw the rolling clouds that sped by.

"It's going to rain." The words were torn from her lips by the wind and whisked away. Adam didn't hear her but kept leading her toward the back of the ship.

When they reached the railing, he halted and turned to face Shauna. He lifted her chin with one finger and slowly bent to claim his kiss. His lips touched hers. For a long moment Shauna felt as if she was floating off the deck, her body light as the wind that whipped by her.

Their lips parted and Adam clutched Shauna to him. She lay her head on his chest and felt the movement of his breathing. Secure arms, she thought, and sighed.

"This trip has been good for me," he said, his voice muffled against her hair.

She leaned her head back and gazed into his eyes, "And for me, too."

She felt his lips touch hers like a whisper, then he placed her at arms length and stared at her.

He turned his gaze from her and looked out across the water. Shauna followed the direction of his eyes and saw the water, an angry green, frothed with whitecaps, beset with large, roiling waves.

For the first time Shauna noticed that the movement of the ship had changed. She clutched the railing to steady herself as the ship fought its way through the huge waves.

He turned back to her and said, "We'd better get inside. It looks like a storm is about to hit."

Shauna noticed one drop, then two fall. She shrugged and laughed. "Too late."

The heavens opened up. Laughing, Adam caught Shauna's arm, and together they ran for the doors. As the glass door shut behind them, Shauna stood and watched the gray sheets of rain pound at the deck. A streak of lightning zigzagged across the sky, illuminating the area where they had stood. She etched the place in her memory.

*Remember his fiancée,* an inner voice said.

No! He's not married yet, she screamed silently. She watched Adam as he studied the world beyond the double doors. The lingering guilt left her as she absorbed each of his features.

Adam met her gaze.

"Will we be all right?" she asked.

A smile lit up his face. "We'll be fine. Just a squall, that's all."

He shook his head and droplets of water rained down upon the wooden deck. Shauna brushed at her shirt and stomped her feet.

"Are we too wet to rejoin the party?" Shauna asked.

He bowed at the waist and answered, "I am fine, if my lady wants an escort to the ball."

Shauna tried to suppress a giggle. "You should have come as a knight. Of course, you might have rusted before making it to shelter a few moments ago."

"And you would be without a handsome, debonair escort for the evening." He held his arm out for her.

She placed her hand upon his forearm, and they walked back into the ballroom. Adam found a secluded spot for them in a corner. They sat and turned their chairs to observe the dancers on the floor.

"Drink?" Adam asked.

Shauna tilted her head in a nod. "A Seven-Up, please."

Adam waved for a waitress, caught her attention, and gave her the order. When he turned back to Shauna, he asked, "Do you want to join the dancers?"

"By myself or with you?"

"Funny. Of course, by yourself." Shauna saw the smile that played at the corners of his mouth as he tried to make his eyes seem serious.

"I'm not dancing alone. Maybe some other time."

"I guess I could assent to one round on the dance floor."

"Well, if it isn't Adam Steele!" A deep voice broke into their conversation.

Shauna stiffened at the sound of the man's voice. She saw Adam stiffen next to her as she swung her gaze up to meet David's.

"I had been meaning to speak to you earlier but just never found the time," David continued, ignoring the hostile stares the two were giving him.

Shauna shot Adam a look and saw the frown set into his features. His next words tore the breath from her, her gaze riveted upon Adam.

"Next month Steele, Inc. should be receiving a large order from us. I'm sure your huge outfit can fill it in no time. Call me when you get back to Dallas. I hate to talk business on a vacation."

Adam's mouth dipped into a deeper frown.

"Good night, Adam, Shauna." David pivoted and strolled from them. A few feet across the room he looked over his shoulder and added, "Sorry I couldn't accommodate you and leave the ship in Jamaica, Adam. I hope Shauna Peters is *nicer* to you than she was to me." David quickly disappeared among the crowd.

Shauna froze. She felt a great pressure in her chest, her face flamed.

"Shauna, let me explain."

She heard the pain in his voice and was disarmed momentarily. No, you couldn't have, came the grim thought. She closed her eyes and inhaled deeply. Tightening her jaw, she clamped down hard to keep her teeth from rattling.

"Shauna."

Her name echoed in the black stillness of her mind. She looked at him as tears filled her eyes.

She raised her hand. "No, don't say any more. Haven't you already made enough of a fool out of me? How could you give me the impression you were just a poor working man? Is that sort of like the poor little rich kid?" Shauna bolted to a standing position and turned her cold stare upon Adam.

"You were the one that assumed I was poor."

She shrank back as she listened to his words.

"I just didn't tell you otherwise," he added.

"For your amusement," she shot back, breathing in quick, shallow gasps.

She fled, blocking from her mind his hand reaching for hers, his voice calling out her name. Running until she found herself in front of the double doors that led to the outside deck, she took one look at the rain pelting the ship and stepped outside. Her tears mingled with the rain that washed over her face. She halted at the bow of the ship and gripped the railing. The vision of Adam haunted her as she stared at the churning sea below. Her mind relived the velvet warmth of his kiss earlier that evening. The hurt sliced deeper as she tried to erase the memory from her mind.

"Fool!" she shouted to the wind. "Love is not for me."

She closed her eyes and felt them burn against her lids. Her clamped lips imprisoned a sob. Work is what is important in life. Hard work, she thought, and choked back the tears that closed her throat.

She opened her eyes and tasted the salt of a tear that tumbled down her cheek. She dashed the wetness of her sorrow from her face, only for it to be replaced with drops of rain. She pushed the red scarf from her head and stepped back against the wall of the ship. Under the overhanging ledge, she watched the rain hammer at the sea, the wind lash at the ship.

A shudder passed through her. Then another one encased her body in chills. She hugged her arms to her and sought the warmer shelter of an enclosed passageway.

Her legs moved automatically toward her cabin. She fumbled for her key in the pocket of her tight pants. When her hand grabbed it, Shauna inserted the key into the lock.

She moved into the dark cabin and felt for the edge of her bunk. She made her way to the head of the bed and eased down onto it, staring into the darkness as thoughts swirled in her mind. David and Adam knew each other! Why didn't he warn me about that man? Visions of that night in David's cabin flashed through her memory. She clenched her hands at her sides.

"That would never have happened if you had just told me about David, Adam," she said aloud. "I wouldn't have been such a fool."

Shauna felt her flesh color as she remembered all the silly things she had told Adam. He must have had a good laugh at my expense, she thought, and gritted her teeth.

"I hope I never see Adam Steele again," Shauna declared to the silent cabin. But her breath was driven from her lungs as a picture of Adam filled her mind.

Shauna huddled deeper under the sheets and hugged her knees to her. She felt icy fingers seep into every pore, drawing the last of her body's warmth from her. Her teeth chattered, her body trembled. She switched on a lamp, eased out of bed, and put on a sweater. Climbing back into her bunk, she closed her eyes and tried to relax, but the chills still encased her in their grip. Finally she dozed.

To Shauna it seemed like only minutes later that she awoke drenched in perspiration. After a glance at her travel clock to see that two hours had passed, she threw back her sheets, took off her sweater and changed into a new nightgown. Wiping her brow with the palm of her hand and lying back on the bed with only her brief gown on, she felt the dampness of her body, the wetness of her bed, and the frizzy tangles of her hair. She sneezed.

"A cold! That's all I need at the end of my beautiful vacation," she muttered into the black stillness.

She rolled over to face the wall and let her eyes close again to continue her sleep. But she tossed and turned the rest of the night only to awake with a jerk the next morning when a knock sounded at her door.

She withdrew a tissue from a box and blew her nose. "Just a minute."

She threw her feet over the edge of the bunk to the floor and slid them into her slippers, jammed her arms into her robe, and trudged to the door. "Who is it?" she asked.

"Adam."

"Go away. I don't have anything more to say to you."

He pounded on the door again. "I won't leave until I can talk with you."

Shauna sucked in her breath, then released it with a loud sigh. "Then say what you came to say and be gone." She heard her bitterness spill over into her voice.

"I won't leave until you open the door and I can talk with you *face to face.*"

Shauna inched the door open and peered out through the crack. "Okay. You have my attention. Speak."

"Not with a piece of metal between us." He pushed on the door. Shauna stumbled backward from the force as he entered the cabin, his face wrinkled with a scowl.

She narrowed her eyes. They glared at each other for a few minutes, each assessing the other's anger.

"I didn't play you for a fool," came his too soft words after the tension had stretched to a breaking point.

"Then why did you lead me on, Mr. Steele?" Shauna planted her hands on her hips and braced her legs apart.

"Shauna, I don't think it's that important if I'm rich

or poor. I am who I am. I have had to live with the fact that I am wealthy most of my life. I chose not to on this trip. I wanted to get away from Dallas and that fact for once in my life."

Shauna straightened. "Well, now you can go back to Dallas and her! You have had your fun. Leave!"

"Yes, now I can go back to her, as you say."

Shauna pivoted and turned her back on Adam. She clenched her jaw tightly to kill the sob in her throat. "Go!" she shouted.

She heard his quick intake of breath, then seconds later the door slamming shut behind her. Her body began to quake uncontrollably. Tears rolled down her cheeks. Her mind burned with the memory of Adam standing not two feet in front of her, his eyes an intense blue, almost black. She could still smell his cologne. His scent permeated the cabin. Shauna took one look in the mirror, saw her alabaster face, and fell upon the bunk, sobbing until there was nothing left inside of her to cry about.

When the alarm on her travel clock rang, Shauna jerked up and fumbled for it, knocking it off the nightstand. She gazed down at the clock as she wiped the tears from her eyes. Ten. Must get going. Last day on board, she thought.

She scanned her wardrobe. "I don't even know if it is still raining," she said aloud as she walked back to the bunk and sat. She picked up the telephone and called information.

"What's the weather like?" she asked, and frowned when she heard the reply. "Raining."

She hung up the receiver and stared at the phone.

"That's all I need. A gloomy day to go along with my gloomy spirits."

Shauna sat watching the rain running down the windowpane. One trail of water merged with another one to form a rivulet of water that raced to the bottom. Shauna blocked all thoughts from her mind except the rain and became mesmerized by the silver drops on the window.

"May I have a seat, dearie?"

Shauna swung her head around to look up at an old lady standing near her. "Huh?"

The woman pointed to the seat on the sofa next to Shauna. "May I sit beside you?"

Shauna moved closer to the arm on the sofa and said, "Oh, yes, of course."

The lady slowly lowered herself onto the sofa, then placed her knitting bag next to her. She took out two needles and a ball of yarn. "I'm knitting some booties for my niece's first baby. She's due any time now."

Shauna smiled at the woman and said, "That's nice," and turned back to watch the rain pelt the window.

"Are you married?"

Shauna stiffened at the question. She twisted around to look at the woman's wrinkled face and shook her head.

"I'm not either, but I have three nephews and four nieces. Making things for them and their families keeps me pretty busy. They paid for this trip. My birthday was last week. I am sixty-four years old." She made her first stitch. "They wanted me to meet some nice gentleman on this cruise. They didn't say it, but I know that was what they were thinking. They are so concerned that I am lonely." She placed her needles in her lap and looked at Shauna. "I am lonely. I live for their visits, but there are no eligible older men on this cruise." The corners of her mouth dipped into a frown. "I wish I had stayed home." She shook her head and stared at the ball of yarn in her lap. "So alone," she whispered, then picked up her needles and began to knit the booties again.

Shauna observed the old lady with her shoulders bent forward, her glasses perched on her nose as she worked on her knitting. Alone. Is that what I am going to be like in forty years? Shauna wondered. Living for other people, waiting for their visits. Her stomach knotted. I don't want to be like her. I want my own family, a husband to grow old with me. Her teeth dug into her bottom lip. Shauna's attention riveted upon the drops of rain.

The high pitch of the old lady's voice penetrated the haze that enveloped Shauna's mind. Shauna saw the woman glance at her watch, then turn its face toward Shauna. "Oh, dear, we only have five minutes till the first seating for dinner." She gathered her knitting together and stuffed it into her large plastic bag. "Do you eat at the first seating, my dear?"

"Yes."

"Then you don't want to be late. Tonight's dinner is supposed to be special since it's the last night. Are you coming?"

Shauna nodded and stood. A war of emotions raged within her as she walked toward the dining room. I can't go in there, she told herself as she saw the doors leading into the dining room. *He* will be in there.

*At the same table!* Panic ignited within her and rapidly spread throughout her body. Every nerve drew as tight as a bowstring. She froze and stared at the doors.

"What's wrong, my dear?" the old lady asked.

Shauna backed away from the woman toward the stairs. "I'm not hungry."

"Aren't you feeling well? You look so pale."

Shauna touched her cheeks, the skin cold beneath her fingertips. She turned and placed her foot on the first step. *You can't run away the rest of your life. Face up to him now and you will be a better person,* an inner voice said.

Shauna brought her foot down next to her other one and turned back to face the old lady. The woman stood slumped over with a worried expression lining her face.

"Should I get the ship's doctor?" the woman asked.

"No. I'm fine . . . now." Shauna strode into the room and scanned the tables. David sat next to the captain. Adam sat next to her empty chair at table number 17. She swallowed hard, squared her shoulders, and took her first step toward her table.

As she passed the captain's table, David smiled at her. He bent his head slightly forward, then turned back to the captain and resumed their conversation.

I've been lucky this trip, she told herself. I've only been burned slightly. It could have been worse. I could be nursing a broken heart. Instead I learned a good lesson. Not to become involved with *any* man.

As she neared table number 17, her heartbeat accelerated. Her legs felt like quickly melting ice. When Shauna placed her hand on the back of her chair and pulled it toward her, she prayed that her hand didn't look like it was shaking, for her body trembled from within. She stepped around from the back of the chair and started to sit, nearly collapsing into the chair as her knees buckled.

Shauna looked up and smiled at the couples around the table, then studied the menu. Adam remained quiet next to her, the silence stretching her nerves even tighter. She jumped when someone nearby cleared his throat, and glancing to the side saw the waiter standing just slightly behind her with his pad and pencil ready to take her order.

Her cheeks turned red. "I'll . . . I'll have this soup and the fruit salad." She pointed to the menu. "To drink I will take a cup of hot tea."

From the corner of her eye she noticed the honeymooners cuddled close together in deep conversation while Mr. Williams and his wife were inspecting the rest of the diners. Shauna avoided looking at Adam.

"Miss Peters, how was your vacation? You certainly have a nice tan," Mrs. Williams said.

Shauna raised her head and looked at the woman. She was at a loss for words. Finally, forcing a smile to her lips, she answered, "I enjoyed all of the ports we called at."

The hairs on Shauna's neck stood out as Adam's stare drilled into her. She twisted the napkin in her lap, then lowered her gaze.

*That's enough, Shauna Peters!* an inner voice chided. *Act happy. Don't let him remember you as a nervous bore.*

Shauna shifted uneasily in her chair, then looked Adam in the eye. "How was your vacation, Mr. Steele?"

His eyes widened slightly before he found the words to answer. "Quite pleasant until last night." His blue eyes became pinpoints as his gaze met hers.

Then he grinned. "Which port did you like the best, *Miss Peters?*"

Her mouth spread into a thin-lipped smile. Her eyes narrowed as her back became ramrod straight. "Possibly the evening I spent in San Juan." She swung her attention to Mrs. Williams and continued, "Could you believe the bargains that St. Thomas had? I spent a fortune there."

Mrs. Williams giggled. "A fortune! I believe we will be indebted for a year because of this trip. I brought an extra suitcase just so I could take all my buys back."

"I wish I'd thought about that," Shauna said.

"We didn't get to town on St. Thomas. We spent most of the day on the beach. The water was so clear and clean," Helen Morris cooed as she leaned closer to her husband and squeezed his hand. They exchanged looks that made Shauna blush.

Shauna was relieved when the waiter brought the first course. Shauna ate her salad and soup in silence, aware of Adam's presence next to her. Once as she reached for the bread basket, Adam's hand brushed hers as he touched the basket at the same time. Shauna let her hand slip away as he handed the basket to her. She smiled her thanks, took a roll, and buttered it.

The waiter opened a bottle of champagne and poured it into wineglasses on the table. "Compliments of the captain," he said.

Shauna downed her drink in three gulps, the bubbly liquid tickling her nose as she brought it to her lips. The liquor warmed her, relaxing her. She leaned back in her chair and watched Mrs. Williams nibble a piece of buttered snail, then wrinkle her nose.

"Ugh, I can't see how the French eat these things." Mrs. Williams pushed the rest of the dish to a far corner of her plate and began to eat her Beef Wellington.

Shauna's stomach contracted at the sight of the rich food on the table. Her head felt dizzy. She took a bite of her roll, not tasting it as she swallowed the bread. The waiter refilled her glass and she gulped the champagne down, the cold liquid soothing her raw throat.

Adam leaned toward her and whispered, "I think you'd better slow down, Shauna."

She shot him a withering stare, then asked the waiter, "May I have another glass of champagne?"

Shauna forced herself to eat and to drink the champagne. He can't tell me what to do, she thought, and finished the last swallow of champagne. She felt lightheaded and blinked.

"Slow down, Shauna," Adam said through clenched teeth.

She turned her narrowed gaze on him. "What I do with my life is no concern of yours, Mr. Steele. If I choose to make a fool out of myself, then I will. I certainly have done a superb job so far." She waved her hand in the air. "Why not now?"

Adam stood and grasped her arm. "Because you're coming with me."

Before she had time to react, Adam had pulled her to her feet and along behind him to the dining room door.

"Stop this instant!" she shouted at him when he had

dragged her through a set of double doors onto the deck.

He halted and Shauna slammed into him. He turned and steadied her.

"Will you take your hands off me!" Shauna glared at the offending hands that gripped her upper arms, then at Adam's face.

"You're such a stubborn woman. Let me explain about this cruise."

"I don't want to hear your explanation. I don't want to . . ."

He crushed her to him and pressed his mouth to hers to quiet her words. Shauna tried to continue to say something, but his kiss turned from a gentle union to a hungry possession. She struggled to free herself, but found her heart betraying her mind as she melted against him.

He picked her up and carried her to a dry deck chair under an overhanging awning. Sitting beside her, he pulled her into the circle of his arms and claimed her lips in another fierce kiss that drove the breath from her lungs.

As his hand caressed a breast, Shauna fought for control of her swirling emotions. She pushed his hand away and leaned away from him.

The hem of her dress whipped about her legs. She brushed strands of hair from her face as she regained control of her breathing.

"Leave me alone. Haven't you done enough to me? Go play your games with someone in your league." She rose to her feet and raced across the deck toward the double doors.

When she reached the safety of her cabin, she threw herself on her bunk and cried until only dry racking sobs sounded in the cabin.

A booming noise startled Shauna. She groaned and rolled onto her side, clasping her hands to her ears, and whispered, "Stop it!"

The ringing persisted. She groped for the phone and knocked the receiver from its cradle. She fumbled for it again and brought it to her ear.

"Shauna, you must get packed. We're docking soon," Adam said.

She licked her dried lips and rasped, "What do you want? I thought I made myself clear last night. Don't you understand English?"

"Get up. You must be packed in thirty minutes. They will pick up your bags then."

She concentrated on his words and slowly the meaning dawned on her. Her eyes widened and she exclaimed, "Oh, my gosh!" She slammed the receiver down and swung her legs to the deck.

"I've never been so glad a vacation is over with. I feel so exhausted and drained. And this cruise was supposed to be relaxing and a good change for me." She stood and walked into the bathroom.

She glanced at herself in the mirror and flinched. Strands of hair went every which way. She had circles under her red, puffy eyes. Her makeup was smeared from her tears. Shauna looked away and ran the cold water and dashed some icy liquid onto her face before she scrubbed it clean.

As she made her way back into the other room, she stared down at her crumpled clothes. I didn't even change into my nightgown, she thought. She ran her hand through her hair and sank into the chair by the closet. He rattles me. He overwhelms me. Thank goodness I'm going back to a sensible job where I can live my life in peace. A hot ache grew in her throat. *He is nothing to me.*

She stared at her empty suitcases. "I can't just sit here all morning. I've got to get packed now," she said aloud.

Shauna pushed herself to a standing position and began to remove her clothes from the closet. She stuffed her luggage full of her new wardrobe—the long gowns, the pantsuits, the shorts. All had been purchased to snare a rich husband. She laughed at the thought.

She took a navy blue pantsuit from the closet, stripped off her wrinkled clothing, and dressed in the suit. Then she closed her suitcases, sitting on one to snap it shut.

She trudged to the door with her bags and placed them outside, making sure that her name tags were on each piece. She climbed the stairs to the Promenade Deck and sat to wait for her letter to be called.

She noticed that one by one people around her began to disembark. Finally the voice over the loudspeaker called out, "P's."

Shauna walked from the ship without a backward glance. Mixed feelings surged through her. She stepped into the customs line and counted the minutes until she stood in front of the customs officer. The man searched one bag, then passed her on through. Shauna sucked in her breath before picking up her luggage and heading toward the doors. She toiled with the heavy bags, stopping every few feet to rest. When she reached the area where the taxi cabs were waiting, she almost dropped each piece of luggage as she placed them on the concrete to wave for a cab.

A driver approached and took her suitcases. He put them into the back of the cab along with several other people's luggage.

"You are going to Miami airport?" the driver asked.

Shauna nodded, climbed into the back seat, and sat next to an elderly couple. The driver slid into the front seat and turned the ignition on. Shauna gazed out the window and inhaled a gulp of air. Not ten feet from her, Adam got into a large black limousine that pulled into the stream of traffic.

Her eyes misted. She choked back her tears and watched the black limousine disappear in the traffic. She would never forget the tall, beautiful woman that hugged Adam and kissed him in the back seat of the limousine. She wished she hadn't seen the two of them. His fiancée, Shauna thought, blinking away the threatening tears. It's over.

*Nothing was ever started, Shauna,* an inner voice said. *You have your own life to live. Forget him.*

Yes, I do have my own life to live. Without Adam, without anyone except myself, she thought. She tilted her chin up, wiped her eyes, and turned to speak to the couple sharing the cab with her.

# Chapter Nine

Mr. Haas sat behind his desk, tapping a pencil on the oak finish. "Very good work, Miss Peters. These last few weeks you have been working much too hard though. I suggest you take the afternoon off. Tomorrow I'll have another client for you."

Shauna stood in front of the large desk, looking down at Mr. Haas. "I can start on the work this afternoon instead of tomorrow morning. I don't have anything to do at home."

The gray-haired lawyer shook his head. "No, Miss Peters, you deserve the day off. I don't ever want to be accused of overworking one of my young lawyers. Now leave and don't show your face in this office until nine tomorrow morning."

Shauna looked at the firm, set jaw, the intense brown eyes, and knew her employer wouldn't take no for an answer. She smiled, turned around, and walked out of his office.

As Shauna went to her small office to retrieve her purse, the phone rang, and she raced to answer it. "Hello, this is Shauna Peters."

"Shauna. It's about time I got hold of you. I've been trying to talk with you since you returned. You're impossible to track down. Are you trying to avoid me? That day I picked you up at the airport you couldn't wait to get home and away from my questions," Nancy said.

"I'm sorry, Nancy, I haven't returned your calls. I've been so busy catching up from my vacation that I just haven't had the time."

"Well, I won't let you think of an excuse this time. I'm coming over to see you tonight."

"Okay. I'll see you for supper at seven."

Shauna hurried to her apartment, put some red beans in a Dutch oven to cook, then kicked off her shoes and propped her feet up on the coffee table. Resting her head on the back of the sofa, she closed her eyes. What am I going to say to Nancy tonight? she asked herself. She'll want to know everything that happened to me—a minute-by-minute account of my trip. Weariness enveloped her as she tried to concentrate on what to say to Nancy. She curled up on the sofa and slept. . . .

Shauna awoke with a start and jolted upright to look around the apartment. It smelled like something was burning. She jumped to her feet, rushed into the kitchen, and yanked the top off the Dutch oven. The water had boiled out of the pot and the red beans were scorched. She pulled the plug out of the socket and dumped the burned dish into the sink. After cleaning the Dutch oven, Shauna glanced at the clock on the wall.

"Six thirty! I guess, Nancy, you'll have to have a tuna fish sandwich for supper," she said aloud.

Shauna padded to the refrigerator and took out the ingredients for the sandwiches. She had finished spreading the tuna fish on the bread when the doorbell rang.

With a wide grin plastered on her face, Nancy strolled into the apartment and said, "Hi. I brought some wine to have with our supper." She sniffed the air. "What happened?"

"I burned the dinner. I hope you like wine with a tuna fish sandwich."

"Tuna fish!" Nancy shrugged. "Oh, well, I'll try anything once."

"Follow me. It's ready if you are."

They walked into the kitchen and Nancy sat at the table. Shauna placed two wineglasses before Nancy. The reporter opened the red wine and filled the glasses. After bringing the plate of sandwiches to the table, Shauna eased into her chair.

Nancy shifted in her seat, took a bite of her sandwich, and said, "I'm ready to hear about your trip. I know something happened by the way you have insisted on remaining silent these last few weeks, but sometimes it's better to talk about it." She placed her chin in the palm of one hand and leaned forward.

Shauna stared at her glass of wine. "Nancy, I would rather forget about the trip."

"It was that bad?"

Shauna's eyes blurred with tears. She nodded, not trusting herself to speak.

"Take a drink of the wine and I'll listen when you're ready." Nancy fell silent as she finished her tuna fish sandwich.

Shauna nibbled on her food and drank a few sips of the wine, but couldn't shake the depression that was overwhelming her. "Maybe you're right. I need to tell someone about it."

Nancy stopped eating and looked up. "Good. I'm all ears."

"I met a man. A wonderful man that played me for a fool. A rich man that was traveling tourist class."

"Shauna, did you do everything I told you?"

Shauna laughed. "Oh, if you only knew the silly things I did do."

Nancy's brow knitted.

Shauna brought her wineglass to her lips and sipped. "Actually I met two rich men, both bachelors."

"And nothing happened?"

"Oh, I didn't say that, Nancy. A lot happened. The first one I met, Adam Steele, was in the taxi I took to the ship. The second rich man I met was David Powell. That was the first night on board the ship."

"Adam Steele of Steele, Inc., based in Dallas, New York, Los Angeles, London, Paris, et cetera?"

Shauna dipped her head in a nod. "The same."

"Why, Shauna, he is very wealthy and *so* handsome. You let him slip through your fingers?"

The color drained from Shauna's face. "He's the one who was traveling like us common folks. I didn't find out who he really was until almost the last day." Shauna lowered her voice and gaze. "He's also engaged to be married soon. I saw the woman and she's everything a man like him needs in a wife."

Shauna watched as Nancy searched her thoughts. "Yes, it seems I read about that a few months ago. Her name is Veronica Blake. She is rich and will inherit a good share of oil stock from her grandfather when she turns twenty-five next year."

"Men like him always turn to their own kind to marry. I wish you'd never talked me into going on that cruise . . . and going along with your foolish plan. At least I'd have some of my self-respect left."

"What in the world did you do?"

"Let's just say I made a complete fool of myself telling Adam I would only marry a rich man, then chasing after David Powell only to find out what kind of man David really is."

Nancy raised her hand. "Hold it. I think I have heard enough, Shauna. Except who is this David Powell?"

"He's from Chicago and owns Powell Industries. He's the one who told me who Adam was."

"He sounds like a nice guy."

Shauna heard the venom that dripped from Nancy's voice. "Oh, he was very nice if you like vipers."

"So now what are you going to do?" Nancy asked and scooted her chair back. She crossed her legs and leaned back.

"Work. What else is there for me to do?"

"I saw Mark yesterday."

Shauna clenched then unclenched her hands. "And how did he look?"

"Medical finals are next month and he didn't look too good. I suppose he has been studying a lot lately, if Catherine allows him to."

Shauna pushed her chair away from the table and leaped to her feet. "Let's talk about something more interesting than Mark or my trip. How was the queen's visit?" Shauna walked from the kitchen to the living room and sat down on the sofa.

Nancy followed her, saying, "Boring, but I did write some good pieces for the newspaper. I'd much rather have been with you on the cruise, but no more about that. Are you working on any interesting cases since your return? Off the record, of course."

"I just wrapped up a tax evasion case and tomorrow Mr. Haas will assign me to another one. Nancy, I want something that will really challenge me."

"Who knows? That may be what Mr. Haas has in mind for you."

Shauna entered Mr. Haas's office and sat in a chair in front of his desk. "You look much better today, Miss Peters. I want you refreshed and ready to go when you meet your next client. He will be joining us shortly, but I wanted to say a few words to you before he arrives. It is very important to make a good impression with this man. His account with this firm will be an extra bonus to us and you. He is a new client who requested your service . . ."

Shauna wiped her palms on the arms of the chair as her heartbeat began to gallop. Then she heard the name Adam Steele and felt the room spin before her eyes. Bolting to her feet, she said, "No! I can't take the case, Mr. Haas!"

She turned to flee when she noticed the doors to Mr. Haas's office open and watched Adam walk into the room. Shauna's gaze riveted upon his face, then moved over him slowly, taking in his dark gray three-piece suit.

Adam strolled forward and extended his hand for Shauna to shake. She acted automatically as she reached out and grasped his. His flesh met hers in a warm clasp. When she recovered from her initial shock, she tried to pull her hand back, but he held it in a viselike hold.

"I have heard so much about you, Miss Peters. It's so good to know you will be handling my tax affairs for this year." He smiled, then let her hand slip to her side.

Mr. Haas indicated a chair in front of his desk for Adam to sit in. Shauna remained standing, watching Adam move to the chair with the grace of a leopard. What is he trying to do to me? she screamed silently.

"Miss Peters, if you will have a seat, we'll discuss Mr. Steele's affairs." Shauna heard the force in Mr. Haas's words and took several steps to her chair. She sat and turned her attention to Mr. Haas, aware of Adam's gaze upon her.

Mr. Haas cleared his throat, then continued, "Miss Peters, Mr. Steele would like you to travel to Dallas for a few weeks to work closely with the accounting department of his corporation. Get to know the business, how the books are set up, et cetera."

Shauna had started to say no when she caught the stern look in Mr. Haas's eyes. Trapped, she thought. She bent her head and studied her hands, folded in her lap. She murmured, "Yes."

"I have arranged for my plane to be ready to leave at

four o'clock sharp for Dallas, Miss Peters," Adam said in a level voice.

"You may have the rest of the day to pack. I'll expect you to be gone for four weeks." Mr. Haas stood and shook Adam's hand. "You have an excellent lawyer, Mr. Steele."

"We shall see," he answered, and shot Shauna a penetrating look as she rose.

"Miss Peters, I have a few things to go over with you before you leave. If you would stay behind for a few minutes, we can take care of it quickly."

"Yes, Mr. Haas."

Adam turned to Shauna and said, "My car will pick you up at three o'clock. I got your address from the secretary. So until three, Miss Peters. Good day." He looked at her intently, then strode to the door.

Shauna watched as he left, all the strength draining from her legs. She sank back into the chair and stared at Mr. Haas.

"Shauna, I get the feeling that you do not care to take on this client. Am I correct?"

Shauna nodded.

"Then I must remind you again that this new account is important to us. Mr. Steele's business interests are extensive. So I expect you to do your best job. I offered my own services, but he insisted on you, so don't let the firm down."

As the numbness began to wear off, she sat straight in the chair and said in a cold voice, "I won't let you down. I have always done my job well and this time will not be any different." She rose. "If that is all, I must see to some things before I leave to pack."

"Very well. I want a progress report from you every week. Good luck." Mr. Haas held his hand out to Shauna. She shook it and left.

When she escaped to the safety of her own office, she fell into her chair and lay her head on her desk. Work for him? I don't understand, she thought. *What kind of game is he playing now?*

Shauna sat in the Lear jet waiting for Adam to arrive. She tapped the arm of her seat, crossed her legs, then uncrossed them. Where is he? she wondered.

The pilot walked through the lounge and stopped by Shauna. "Mr. Steele has just pulled up. We'll be taking off in a few minutes. Would you please fasten your seat belt now, Miss Peters?"

Shauna fumbled with the buckle and finally snapped herself into the seat. As the pilot turned to leave, she called out, "Is Mr. Steele on board the plane?"

"Yes," the pilot replied, then left.

Shortly afterward Shauna heard the roar of the engines as the ignition was turned on.

"Why isn't he back here with me?" she whispered, and looked out the window. She noticed that the plane was moving toward the runway and felt a tightness in her chest.

Shauna leaned back in her seat and closed her eyes. She gripped the arms of the seat, her knuckles turning white. Think about something other than takeoff, she told herself. She relived the moment when the chauffeur had knocked on her door and blushed when she remembered the face she had made as she flung open the door, expecting to see Adam, but instead seeing the driver standing in the doorway. The words she was going to say to Adam flew from her mind as she stammered, "Come in."

In her mind's eye Shauna again could see the driver walking into the apartment, taking the bags, and asking if she were ready to go. She could remember the cold shiver that spread over her at the brisk manner of the driver. Like Adam this morning, she thought.

As Shauna felt the gravitational pull when the plane took off, her fingernails dug deeper into the cushioned arms of the seat. When the plane leveled off, she opened her eyes and stared into the smiling face of Adam, sitting across from her.

He dipped his head slightly and said, "My pilot is very good. We haven't had a crash . . . yet."

Shauna heard the amusement that laced each of his words. She turned her head and looked out the window. Puffs of white clouds sped by with patches of blue peeking out from them.

"We have to make a slight detour because of a storm system moving into the New Orleans area, but we won't be too late arriving in Dallas."

"I really don't care when we get there, so long as we get there in one piece." Shauna continued to stare out at the quickly darkening sky.

"Shauna, about the cruise . . ."

Shauna twisted around to face Adam. Her eyes narrowed as a frown creased her face. "No, Adam—or rather, Mr. Steele. I work for you as your tax lawyer and that is all we'll discuss between us." Shauna shook her head. "I don't know why you wanted me for your lawyer when I know for a fact there are some excellent ones in Dallas, but I'm going to be your tax lawyer for as long as you want. Mr. Haas made that quite clear to me. I don't like being forced into anything, but I will do a good job. That you can count on."

Adam's blue eyes became pinpoints as he slowly spoke. "I'm paying your firm a lot of money, so you'd better do more than a good job." He stood, his arms stiff at his sides. "I have some work to do in my office, so if you will excuse me, I'll return to it." He strode from the lounge.

Shauna saw streaks of lightning light the black clouds to the east. Her breath caught in her lungs as she heard the distant rumble of thunder. For hours she sat tense, scanning the heavens, praying.

When the plane finally landed in Dallas three hours later, Shauna's legs felt weak as she stepped off the plane and was guided by Adam to a waiting car. His grip on her elbow loosened when she slid into the back seat. He climbed in next to her and tapped on the glass window separating the driver from them.

The car moved forward. For forty-five minutes they rode toward Dallas in strained silence. Adam studied the countryside out one window while Shauna gazed out the other.

"I have arranged for you to stay at one of the company's apartments near our office building. I'll drop you off there before going home."

"How kind of you, Mr. Steele. Is this one of the fringe benefits you offer the people who work for you?"

Shauna heard his quick intake of breath. The air became even thicker with tension.

"I'm a relatively patient man, Miss Peters, but I must

warn you that when I do lose my temper I am hard to control."

She looked in his direction. "Thanks for the warning. Since I've already experienced being the object of your amusement, I suppose being the object of your temper won't be much different."

"Don't bet on it," came the harsh reply.

Silence.

When the car halted in front of an apartment building, Adam said, "The driver will show you to your apartment." He folded his arms across his chest, leaned his head back, and closed his eyes.

Shauna seethed with mounting rage. She glared at him for a moment before climbing out of the car. The same brisk chauffeur as in New Orleans escorted her to the penthouse suite. He unlocked the door, handed her the key, and placed the bags inside the door.

He tilted his hat and said, "Good night, Miss Peters."

Shauna walked into the entrance hall of the apartment and gasped. The living room was huge with a sliding glass door and full-length windows along one wall that led to a balcony. Shauna's gaze took in the well-stocked bar along half of another wall and the two long, blue velvet sofas arranged near the fireplace. She walked several steps into the room, her shoes sinking into the plushness of the white carpet. The drapes were pulled back to emit the last rays of the setting sun, casting a warm orange glow on the walls.

She noticed a woman walking in from the dining room. "You must be Miss Peters. I am Pat Davis, the housekeeper. Let me help you with your luggage and show you to your bedroom. Dinner will be served anytime you are ready." Pat offered Shauna a wide grin as she bent to carry the two suitcases down the hallway to the right into a bedroom.

Shauna followed the large woman as she waddled through the doorway into a sitting room. Pat glanced over her shoulder and said, "The bedroom is through that door. Do you want me to help you unpack?"

Shauna stood motionless in the middle of the sitting room, trying to absorb all the luxury before her. She wanted to kick off her shoes and run her toes through the carpet. She wanted to relax on the couch. But instead she strolled into the bedroom behind the housekeeper and surveyed the room, which was dominated by a king-size four-poster bed. A rich, satin spread covered the bed with a matching canopy draped above it. Shauna placed her purse on the dresser, then walked into the bathroom.

She stood frozen in the doorway as her gaze traveled over the sunken bathtub, the sauna, the faucets of brass, the stark white tile and accents of green splashed throughout the room. I'm in another world, she thought.

"What time would you like your supper, Miss Peters?"

Shauna turned and looked at the housekeeper. "Call me Shauna, please. I think I'll eat something light—say in about thirty minutes. I'll unpack and be in the kitchen then."

Pat tilted her head in a nod and left the room. Shauna stared again at the bedroom with its white carpet and green draperies. She moved to a green velvet chair and sank into it, removed her shoes, and wiggled her toes in the lush pile of the carpet. Well, you'd better enjoy the finer things in life while you can, she told herself. At least until you find out what Adam is trying to do.

# Chapter Ten

"I trust the apartment is to your liking," Adam said as he sat behind his desk. He placed a stack of letters to the side and rested one elbow on the desk blotter, cupping his chin in the palm of his hand as he examined Shauna. "You don't look well. Was the bed too hard? Did Miss Davis talk to you until the wee hours of the morning?"

Shauna's mouth spread in a tight smile. "I came here to do a job, not to be cross-examined about what I do with my free time." She leaned forward in the chair and said in a controlled voice, "Now if you'll tell me where I'm supposed to start my job, I'll get busy."

"First, I'd like to take you on a tour of the building. I want you to familiarize yourself with the layout of the company. Then I'll introduce you to the head accountant." Adam rose and walked from behind his desk. He took Shauna's arm and helped her to her feet.

Motioning with his hand, he said, "This way, Miss Peters."

A few steps across Adam's office Shauna halted. "I know you're my employer *for the moment,* but I can walk by myself . . . without your assistance." Shauna's gaze shot to the hand that touched her arm. His fingertips seared her flesh.

She saw his jaw quiver as he brought his arm to his side. A vein in his neck throbbed when she backed away. The heavy silence charged the air as Shauna watched Adam fight to control his emotions.

"It seems I remember you telling me once before you didn't need my assistance." He turned and strode to the door. Over his shoulder he called, "If you're coming, I suggest you get a move on."

Shauna followed Adam from his office and down the hallway. They visited department after department until two hours later, with sore feet, Shauna was standing in front of the head accountant.

"Mr. Ripley, this is Miss Peters. She will work with you on preparing the tax statement for this year."

Shauna smiled at the little man with only a rim of brown hair around his head. They shook hands. "It's good to meet you, Mr. Ripley."

"And you."

"Well, if you two will excuse me, I must return to my office." Adam walked to the door, then glanced back and said, "By the way, Miss Peters, I forgot to ask you to the company party that is being held at my house tomorrow evening. Mr. Ripley will inform you about any details you may need to know." He thrust the door open and vanished before Shauna could voice her protest.

Shauna swung her gaze to Mr. Ripley. She raised her eyebrows and asked, "Company party?"

"It is held every year about this time at Mr. Steele's estate. He invites everyone working in the main office as well as key personnel at the branch offices." Mr. Ripley indicated a chair for Shauna. He sat in one across from her. "It is a big, fabulous affair that starts at eight o'clock and goes till . . ."

"Till?"

"Until early morning sometimes. We are closed the next day as a bonus to the employees and we get a long weekend to recuperate from the gala."

"My, it sounds interesting." Her voice dripped with sarcasm. "Of course, I won't go to the affair. I'm only working here temporarily."

"You will be missing quite a party. This year Miss Blake will be there. Everyone is dying to meet the woman who finally snared Mr. Steele. I nearly won the company pool on when Mr. Steele would get married. His wedding, I hear, is being planned for next September. Nothing official, so don't mention it to him. If he had only waited another few months, I would be one hundred dollars richer."

Shauna's eyes grew wide. "You bet on when he would marry?"

"Some of the employees started the pool two years ago. Everyone put up one dollar and received a year and month."

"Does Mr. Steele know about it?"

Mr. Ripley shook his head. "Oh, no. Heavens, he would be furious."

"Who is this Miss Blake?"

Mr. Ripley appeared to choose his words carefully.

"She is rich and beautiful. Actually I have only seen her once in the lobby with Mr. Steele. But I have heard . . ." Mr. Ripley bit his lower lip and rose. He strode to his desk and picked up a manila folder.

"Heard what?"

He glanced at her quickly and said, "Oh, nothing. As I said, I know little about her except that she is rich and beautiful. Now let's look over the figures for . . ."

I won't go tomorrow night, Shauna told herself. I can't meet *her*. Adam loves *her* not me. Me? . . . *I love Adam.* I want Adam for me, not her. Shauna stared through Mr. Ripley. I love Adam, she repeated to herself, somewhat amazed at the realization. A man who is beyond my reach! She let her gaze drop to the floor as her heart constricted and the tears welled within her eyes. What am I going to do now? How can I be near him and never be able to touch him, to kiss him?

Shauna stared at the green canopy above her. The doorbell rang but she remained on the bed, tracks of tears drying on her cheeks. She rolled over and closed her eyes. Pictures of Adam in his clown suit, of Adam rescuing her from David flashed across her mind. She squeezed her eyes shut tighter and whispered, "Leave me be!"

"Shauna, are you awake?" came the whispered question.

Shauna propped herself up on her elbows and looked at Pat. "Yes."

Pat hesitated to speak as she shifted from one foot to the other.

"What is it?"

"Mr. Steele's driver is here to pick you up for the

party . . . I . . . I, er . . ." She cleared her throat and continued, "I told him you weren't going."

"And is he gone now?"

Pat's head sagged forward as she murmured, "No."

"Why not? I don't like that man anyway. Didn't he understand you when you told him I wasn't going?"

Pat's gaze met Shauna's. "Yes, he understood, but his orders are not to return without you."

Shauna bolted from the bed and stomped across the room. "We'll just see about that." She entered the entrance hall with a grim expression set deep into her features. In a tight, slow voice she said, *"I am not going to the party.* You can tell *your* Mr. Steele anything you want *but I am not going.* Is that understood?"

The driver squared his shoulders. "I'm not leaving until you accompany me to Mr. Steele's house. I have my orders from Mr. Steele." His tone was harsh, inflexible.

Shauna stomped her foot and balled her hands. She stood ramrod straight and glared into the driver's face. "Leave this instant!"

Silence.

"I'll call the police if you don't."

"And tell them what? This apartment is owned by Mr. Steele, not you. All they would do is laugh at you."

Shauna felt the color drain from her face. "But I don't feel well."

The driver's gaze flickered over Shauna before he said, "You look fine to me." He leaned against the door and studied his fingernails.

"Oh!" Shauna stormed back to her bedroom, calling over her shoulder, "Help me dress, Pat."

The housekeeper scurried into the room, her large

frame moving surprisingly quickly. "What do you want to wear?"

"Oh, anything. I don't care. No, wait. I know." Shauna walked to the closet and took a pair of jeans from a hanger, then a wine-colored velour shirt with large bell sleeves. "I will wear these."

"But the party is formal."

A devilish grin played at the corners of Shauna's mouth. "I know, but Mr. Steele should learn to relax, wear comfortable clothes."

Shauna slipped her robe off and dressed in the jeans and shirt. She stepped into her shoes and ran a comb through her hair. "I'm ready. How do I look?"

Pat gulped. "Not exactly like someone I would expect to show up at one of Mr. Steele's parties." Pat threw her arms up in the air and said, "You'd better change, Shauna."

Shauna moved her head from side to side. "No way. If he wants me at this gala so badly, then he must take me as I am. I'll tell you all about the affair tomorrow morning. I expect I will be back early. Good night, Pat." Shauna grabbed a jacket, left her room, and made her way to the entrance hall.

If the driver noticed that her clothes were unusual, Shauna could not tell when his gaze traveled the length of her body. Shauna observed the driver's appraisal, then tilted her chin up, and walked out of the apartment. Her pride flared. I will not be bullied by anyone, not even Adam Steele, she thought.

The long drive out to Adam's estate gave Shauna time to think. Her doubts about her attire rose within her and plagued her during the journey through the countryside.

About halfway there, she leaned forward and started to tap on the glass separating her from the driver. No! You have committed yourself to this course of action whether you like it or not, Shauna Peters, she whispered to herself, and sat back against the seat.

*But what if he complains to Mr. Haas?* an inner voice asked.

Then I must face that situation when it arises, she told herself. I am a good lawyer and can get a job with another firm if I have to. Or perhaps I can open my own law office.

The car turned into a long driveway flanked by large oak trees with branches that formed a canopy over the drive. When Adam's house appeared in her view, Shauna's breath caught in her throat. A large, brown stone mansion lay before her. They passed rows of cars parked along the driveway until they pulled up in front of the house. A car attendant hopped up from his chair to open the car door for Shauna. She climbed out and caught the startled expression in the attendant's eyes. She smiled, straightened to her full height, and watched the boy regain his composure and hurry to open the double front doors for her.

When Shauna stepped into Adam's house, she walked into a large entrance hall with a marble floor and a winding staircase. Her gaze was drawn to the three-tiered crystal chandelier that lit the hall.

"May I take your . . . your jacket?" she heard a haughty voice say next to her.

Shauna turned her head and looked into cold brown eyes. "Thank you," she replied sweetly to the butler, and slipped the jacket off her arms.

Shauna heard voices drifting from the rooms on all

sides of the hallway. She shot a questioning look at the butler as he walked past her toward one of the rooms.

"This way, Miss. I assume you were invited to the party." He threw her a look over his shoulder that conveyed his doubts.

Shauna chuckled. "Yes. Mr. Steele even sent his chauffeur to pick me up."

Shauna saw his brows knit and suppressed her giggles by swallowing hard. A foot behind the butler, Shauna entered the living room filled with people, all dressed in tuxedos or long evening gowns. Suddenly Shauna's courage fled as her gaze rested upon Adam's face, a face of stone with two pools of ice staring at her. She clenched her hands at her sides and made her way to her host.

When she stepped in front of Adam, she felt all the eyes in the room on her. Everyone around him except the tall, beautiful creature from the pier at Fort Lauderdale moved a good distance away from them. Shauna met his wintry stare with her own.

A smile was carved on her face as she spoke. "It was so good of you to send your driver to pick me up."

His gaze raked down her body, then returned to look her in the eye. "It was the least I could do, since you don't know your way around Dallas."

Shauna inclined her head slightly, then turned her gaze upon the woman next to Adam. Shauna offered her hand and said, "I'm Shauna Peters."

The woman looked at the gesture of friendship, then at Shauna. She reluctantly shook Shauna's hand. "I am Veronica Blake."

Shauna heard the voice that was as smooth as velvet with a touch of frost in it and tensed.

"Miss Peters is the tax lawyer I hired recently," Adam said as he moved closer to Miss Blake. He looked down at Veronica. "But I believe she doesn't know what formal attire means."

Shauna almost choked and gritted her teeth together as she replied, "And I believe you don't know how to accept no as an answer."

Shauna heard a few people suck in their breaths. She saw daggers of hate in Veronica's green eyes and the bitter twist of Adam's mouth.

Her courage returned to surge through her veins. "If you would just ask your driver to take me back to the apartment, you will be rid of this offending attire."

The air became charged with electricity. Not a word was spoken, not a sound made until Adam threw back his head and laughed. The tension in the room eased as his laughter roared from his throat.

"When you are accustomed to getting your own way, it's hard to accept no for an answer." He bowed at the waist. "Forgive me, Miss Peters."

The corners of Shauna's mouth curled into a smile. "You are forgiven, Mr. Steele."

"Then allow me to show you my house." Adam turned to Veronica and said, "I'll be back in a while, darling." He touched Veronica's arm briefly before moving next to Shauna and taking her hand.

As Shauna walked from the room with Adam, she felt her skin tingle from Veronica's piercing stare and the questioning looks of the other guests.

Shauna allowed Adam to lead her from the house into the rose garden with a waterfall that tumbled into a pool. The rosy hue of the sunset cast a glow over the water. Bushes and bushes of every color of rose were sprinkled throughout the garden with the stone pool in the center.

Shauna stood near the pool looking at the vivid colors that surrounded her. She took a quick breath and released it. "Adam, this is heavenly. This pool is more like a pond than what I would call a pool. And roses are my favorite flowers!"

"I guessed they might be. That's why I sent you that yellow rose on the cruise."

Shauna snapped her head around to look at Adam. "You sent it!"

He nodded.

She stiffened. "Well, thank you . . . a month late." She compelled herself to smile and stepped a few feet sideways to touch a yellow bud. "I like it here in this garden."

Without a word Adam pulled Shauna toward a bench under a large oak tree. Within the shade of the oak, Shauna sat and searched the dark shadows to read Adam's expression. A blank mask greeted her appraisal.

"Don't you think you should get back to your guests?" Shauna felt his hand grasp hers. She jerked hers back and gripped the edge of the stone bench. The coolness of the stone soothed her taut nerves.

"Shauna, I want to explain about the cruise, and you are going to let me this time." Shauna heard the frustration that cut through his words.

She nodded, not trusting herself to speak.

"I wasn't playing games with you. For one short week—or almost one week—I forgot who I was. I was just plain Adam Steele, another guy enjoying himself on a vacation. I wasn't a man who runs a multimillion-dollar corporation, who has always had people falling all over themselves to please him. And frankly, Shauna, I enjoyed myself for the first time in a long while. I didn't think *anyone* needed to know who I was."

"I'm glad you enjoyed slumming. I guess it can have its amusements to someone who knows he will go back to a large mansion in the country." Shauna spread her arms out before her. "And to toying with people's lives." She rose to her feet. "Adam, I no longer blame you for not telling me who you really were. As you have pointed out—indirectly, of course—it isn't my business. It's unimportant to our lives what happened on that cruise. You have returned to your mansion. I have returned to my job. It's as simple as that." She stared a few more brief seconds at Adam, then spun around and fled through the garden into the house.

She felt her heart race, the blood pulsating through her veins as she escaped up the stairs and into a vacant bedroom. She closed the door behind her and leaned against the wood. Shauna looked down at her trembling hands and clutched them to her heaving chest. A sob tore from her throat. "Oh, Adam, if only things were different," she cried, and let the tears flow. Shauna made her way to a chair and fell into it. She buried her face in her hands and wept. A minute ticked into minutes as she felt an emptiness take hold of her.

From a distance she heard approaching voices. She yanked her head up and listened. The voices became louder and louder, then began to fade as the people passed the door and moved on down the hall.

*You can't lose control here of all places. You don't want anyone to walk in on you crying,* an inner voice said.

She dashed the tears from her cheeks, walked to the dresser, and withdrew a tissue from a box. Her red, blotchy face met her gaze in the mirror.

She ran her fingers across her cheeks and whispered, "Oh, no! Everyone will know I have been crying— especially Adam and that Veronica."

Shauna strode into the bathroom and splashed cold water onto her face and examined herself again, smiling this time. "Not too bad. I'll just wait a few more minutes before returning downstairs."

She stepped back into the bedroom and stopped dead in her tracks.

"Well, I had no idea you were in here," Veronica said in a too-sweet voice.

"I'm sure you didn't. I was just leaving." Shauna started to move toward the door.

Shauna saw Veronica walk to the dresser and open her purse. She patted the tip of her nose with a powder puff and rearranged a few strands of her jet black hair. "Don't leave on my account. I would love to get better acquainted with someone who *works* for Adam." She swept around and let her gaze travel the length of Shauna. "Wherever did you find the courage to wear such . . . such a novel outfit?"

Shauna noticed the small turned-up nose wrinkle slightly. Shauna stood straighter and leveled a penetrating gaze at Veronica. "Whoever gave you the right to question my attire?"

Veronica's green eyes flashed fire. She touched her

left hand and twisted a ring around her finger. "This, my dear. Adam's mine and I hope you'll not forget it. I would hate to see a nice girl like you get hurt playing a game when she doesn't know the rules." Veronica then gave Shauna a wide smile and brushed past her to the door, throwing a glance over her shoulder that was full of her contempt. "I saw that look in your eyes when you spoke to Adam. Don't get the idea a man like Adam would ever fall for someone out of his class." She opened the door and left.

Shauna stared at the closed door, her mouth slightly opened. How dare she threaten me, she thought after a few moments of silence. Now I think I know what Mr. Ripley wanted to say. Veronica Blake is an unpleasant and malicious woman!

Again Shauna heard voices outside the door. The door swung open and two women, laughing, entered the room. When they saw Shauna, they stopped and stared at her.

Shauna felt her temper rise under their scrutiny. She raised her chin in determination and said in a cold voice, "I was just leaving. If you'll excuse me, *ladies.*"

When Shauna shut the door behind her, she heard the giggles of the two women, and one of them said, "So that's the one. Veronica is certainly right about her."

Shauna straightened and began to walk toward the stairs with her arms stiff at her sides. At the top of the landing she met Mr. Ripley and smiled at the older man.

He nodded and said, "You have caused quite a stir,

Miss Peters." He chuckled. "But I think you look fine. Comfortable." Mr. Ripley put his finger in his collar and pulled on it. "These tuxedos are always so tight around the neck for me."

"Thank you, Mr. Ripley. That's the first kind word I have received all evening. I trust I'll get to meet your wife before the evening is over."

"Oh, yes. She is dying to meet you. I arranged for us to sit next to each other at dinner."

"Then, till dinner." Shauna descended the stairs with him and started to enter the living room.

"Miss Peters."

Shauna turned and faced Adam. She drew her brows together in a frown. "Yes, Mr. Steele?"

"I haven't finished giving you a tour of the house."

"I have seen quite enough, Mr. Steele. Frankly, everything I have seen is a bit too much for me."

He raised an eyebrow. "For someone who wanted to marry a rich man so she wouldn't have to worry about her future, that's an odd statement."

"Women can change their minds." She swept past him and strode toward the living room as everyone else was moving toward the dining area. Mr. Ripley was standing back from the group waving at her. She walked toward him, relief washing over her. At least I'm not completely alone, she thought.

"Miss Peters, I would like you to meet my wife, Ruth."

"It's so good to know someone will talk with me. My name is Shauna."

Ruth gripped Shauna's hand in a firm handshake. "Tom has told me so much about you in the last two days. He says you're brilliant. I just had to meet the woman he called brilliant, since he rarely gives a compliment to anybody."

Shauna looked at Mr. Ripley. She noticed his reddened face and smiled. "I hope in the next few weeks I can live up to his expectations."

Ruth gave Shauna a warm smile and said, "For some reason I feel you will."

Tom cleared his throat. "Well, ladies, if we don't get started, we'll miss dinner."

Shauna tucked her hand through Mr. Ripley's arm on one side while his wife took his other arm. They made their way into the dining area and searched for their places.

Shauna turned a puzzled face to Tom. "I thought you said that I would be seated next to you and your wife. The name on this card is Marie Carson."

Tom's brows furrowed. "But I did arrange it earlier tonight." He shrugged. "I don't know what to say."

Shauna sensed someone move to stand beside her. She twisted around to see Adam next to her.

"As a guest of my company, I thought it only proper that you sit at the head table with me."

"But I would rather be with Mr. Ripley and his wife." Shauna spoke with an urgency.

In a harsh whisper Adam said, "Remember, Shauna, I'm a man who doesn't know how to accept no for an answer." His lips stretched into a tight grin as he extended his arm for Shauna to take.

Shauna saw the flash of hatred in Veronica's eyes as they approached the head table. Through clenched teeth she whispered, "Don't you think you should have cleared this arrangement with your fiancée? She doesn't look too happy about me sitting next to you."

Adam's gaze met hers. "That's her problem. She must learn to curb her jealous tendencies. I work closely with many beautiful women in the course of one day. She will have to learn to bear it."

Shauna drew in a quick breath. "Don't you ever get jealous?" She shook her head. "My, Adam, you are a cold person. Why didn't I ever see that on the cruise?"

"Perhaps it was the warmer climate that melted my icy barrier for a brief week." He pulled Shauna's chair out for her and she slipped into it.

"Then I suggest you move your main office to Miami." She forced her mouth into a smile as she batted her eyes at him.

Through each course Shauna felt alone as she listened to the conversations around her. Veronica with her too-sweet voice monopolized Adam with her plans on what she would do to his house once she became Mrs. Steele. Shauna tried to ignore them, but she kept finding herself drawn to their conversation.

As Shauna ate the last piece of her filet mignon, Adam turned to her and said, "Are you enjoying the party?"

"I'm enjoying this evening about as much as I enjoyed the evening in David's cabin."

"That much! Perhaps you'd like to leave after the dinner? Dessert will be served in a few minutes."

"Adam, I would like to have left two hours ago. When I arrived."

He inclined his head. "I was wrong in making you come here. I wanted to explain my side of the trip as well as have you see my home."

Shauna turned to look at Adam in the eye. "How could this be a home? A house perhaps, but not a home. It's too big. This house has almost as many bedrooms as some hotels I've been in."

Adam's blue eyes turned almost black as they narrowed and glared at her. "What would you know about this house? I was raised here and never wanted for a thing."

One of the waiters brought Shauna her dessert and saved her from replying. She took a bite of the chocolate soufflé and chewed it slowly as it melted in her mouth. She felt Adam's gaze upon her for several more bites before from the corner of her eye Shauna saw him turn his attention back to Veronica. Shauna released her pent-up breath and ate the rest of the dessert, relishing the sweet taste.

As people stood and began to drift into the ballroom, Shauna faced Adam and said, "I'd like to go home now. Can you have your driver take me back to the apartment?"

"Only on one condition, Shauna."

She planted her hands on her waist. "And what's that?" she asked in an exasperated voice.

"That you dance with me . . . just one dance."

Shauna set her features in a frown and nodded. Adam stood and held his hand out to her. She grasped his hand and he led her into the ballroom and out onto the dance floor. Couples surrounded them as the floor filled with people. The music blared across the space, Shauna moving her body to the fast tempo. Suddenly, she heard the song fade and a soft, slow tune drift over the couples on the dance floor. Adam pulled her into his arms and held her closely against him. One hand lay across her back, rubbing the muscles into relaxation until she was limp. They turned and stepped around the floor. The music encased her in its softness. Her earlier tension poured from her. She closed her eyes and thought of the love that had gone into the writing of the song. Each note held the passion of the writer within it.

When the music stopped, Shauna clung to Adam. His hand was still massaging her back and his face was still buried in her hair.

"You smell wonderful, Shauna."

He spoke her name softly. His breath caressed her neck. A shiver bolted through her body and she nestled closer within his embrace.

Shauna sensed the other couples leave the dance floor and opened her eyes as she pulled away. Glancing around the room, she caught Veronica staring at her. A shudder squirmed down her spine.

"Now, may I go?" Shauna asked and flinched at the hardness in her voice.

Adam bowed. "Of course. I'm a man of my word."

He guided her from the floor. She pulled her hand from his grasp and followed him toward the front doors.

As Shauna passed Veronica, Veronica stepped closer to her and whispered, "Remember, he's mine. Little girls that play with matches get burned."

# Chapter Eleven

A ringing noise invaded Shauna's dream and brought her into the bright world of morning. Blinking her eyes as the sunlight streaked across the bedroom and fell upon her face, she turned over and squeezed her eyes shut. The ringing persisted. She yanked the pillow next to her over her head.

Moaning and fully awake, Shauna eased the pillow from her head and threw it across the bed. A soft knock tapped at her door. She sat up and asked, "Yes?"

"Mr. Steele is here to see you, Shauna."

Shauna brought the sheet up to her chin and hugged it to her. "Tell him to go away. This is my day off."

"If you want me to go away you must tell me to my face. Otherwise I will camp out in your living room and wait," Adam shouted from the hallway.

"You'll have to wait an awfully long time," she shouted back.

"It's my day off also, and I have all the time in the world to wait for you."

Shauna glared at the door. "That man! Can't he leave me in peace!" she muttered as she slipped out of bed. Jamming her arms through the sleeves of her robe, she stomped to the door and thrust it open to stare into the smiling face of Adam as he leaned against the wall.

"Good morning," he said in a too-cheerful tone.

"What's good about it? I got to bed late and I got up too early, thanks to a certain party on both accounts." Shauna braced her legs apart and planted her hands on her hips. "Well, I am telling you to your face to go now!"

"Okay, but first get dressed and have breakfast with me. I told Pat to fix us a large breakfast. I'm starved."

"Well, I'm not." She turned to close the door.

"Please, Shauna, grant me this one favor." Adam stepped forward and touched her arm.

Shauna felt his fingers on her arm and nearly fell against him. Her wall of indifference began to crumble.

"I would like to talk with you."

Shauna glanced over her shoulder. "Why?"

"I enjoyed our conversations on the cruise. I just want to talk about anything, nothing." Adam's hand slipped to his side.

She heard the pleading tone in his voice and felt her heart twist. Her shoulders slumped forward slightly as she finally said, "Okay. I'll be out in a few minutes."

She listened to Adam's footsteps retreating from her bedroom and her heartbeat matched his quick pace. Bringing her trembling hand up to brush her hair from her face, she whispered, "Oh, Adam."

Shauna stood by the door a moment longer, then hurried to dress, donning a pair of old jeans and a T-shirt. She ran a comb through her hair, then slid her feet into a pair of sandals.

When she appeared in the living room, Adam rose from the couch and watched her enter. A tremor shot up her spine as his gaze followed her every move. A slow blush spread over her.

"Please don't stare at me so," she said as she walked with him toward the balcony.

"I asked Pat to set the table on the terrace. It's such a beautiful spring morning."

Shauna stepped out onto the balcony and took a deep breath. The air smelled clean and fresh. The bright sunlight warmed her. She sat in the chair Adam pulled out for her and raised both eyebrows as she looked into his eyes.

"I guess old habits die hard."

"That's okay. I think I enjoy things being done for me. All my life I have done for myself. It's nice for a change to have someone do for me." Shauna sipped her orange juice and examined Adam over the rim of her glass.

She trapped his gaze with hers. Time crawled by. Then suddenly his gaze dropped to the table. She watched as he buttered a piece of toast.

"I had hoped you would return with me to the house and swim. It's a lovely day." Adam waved his arm up toward the cloudless sky.

"Adam, I hardly think it would be a lovely day fending off hostile remarks by Veronica. I believe I prefer staying here and reading a good mystery."

Adam reached across the table and clasped her hand

within his. "Shauna, I'm not blind. You may think me a fool but not blind. I know how Veronica feels, and she won't be at the house. She had to travel to Houston for a few days."

"And while the cat is away the mouse will play. Is that it, Adam?" Shauna leaped to her feet and through narrowed slits looked at Adam. "I won't be a part of some game you want to play to amuse yourself while Veronica is out of town." She pivoted and stalked toward the sliding glass door.

He grabbed her arm and spun her around. "Amuse myself with! Do you think that is all I want to do with you?" His eyes were pinpoints, boring into her flesh.

She lifted her chin in defiance. "Yes. Why else do you seek my company behind your fiancée's back?"

Adam opened his mouth to speak, then clamped it shut. His gaze drilled into every inch of her face. Finally he spoke in a deadly quiet voice. "I'm beginning to wonder that myself." He dropped her arm and backed away. He bowed and said, "Good day, Miss Peters. I hope you enjoy your mystery." She watched him walk from the terrace through the living room to the front doors.

Shauna heard herself shout to Adam, "Wait!"

He halted and slowly turned.

With a will of their own, Shauna's legs carried her across the living room to stand in front of Adam. "I'm sorry. I didn't sleep well last night and my disposition is suffering for it today." She offered him a smile. "Yes, I would like to go to your house for a swim, but I didn't bring a suit. It's still April and a bit cold for swimming."

"I have a suit that will fit you at the house and my

pool is heated. I've been swimming in it since the first of March."

"Then if you will wait I'll get my purse and be with you in just a minute." Shauna hurried to the bedroom and picked up her purse and a sweater.

When she reappeared in the hallway, Adam was gone. She searched the living room and balcony, but he was nowhere to be seen. Then she heard voices floating from the kitchen, laughter filling the air.

Shauna walked through the dining room into the kitchen and noticed Adam and Pat sitting at the table drinking coffee and laughing. Adam looked up and motioned for Shauna to join them.

"I hadn't had a chance to talk with Pat in a long time and thought I would say hello before leaving."

"More coffee?" Pat held the pot up to pour some of the steaming brew into Adam's cup.

Adam shook his head. "This is my fourth cup this morning and I think I am awake."

Shauna laughed. "You'd better be. Remember, you're driving me to your house and that is a good thirty-minute drive. I would hate to see you fall asleep at the wheel." Shauna sat in the empty chair next to Adam and poured herself a cup of coffee. She added cream and sugar to the chocolate-colored liquid. As she stirred the coffee, she gazed into Adam's eyes and saw the intense look he gave her. She smiled, but a lump grew in her throat making it impossible for her to talk.

She listened as Pat spoke. "Shauna, you wouldn't believe the things that Adam used to do when he was growing up."

Shauna drew her brows together in puzzlement.

"I used to work at the house for Adam's parents. I

helped in the kitchen, and there were many nights that I sneaked food up to Adam because he had been sent to bed without supper." Pat giggled. "That was naughty of me, but I could never resist Adam's pleas for help. All he had to do was flash those big blue eyes at me and I would melt. I remember once . . ."

Those big blue eyes, Shauna thought. Yes, Pat, I know what you mean. I melt every time I look at him and die every time I think of Veronica in his embrace.

Adam placed his hand on her arm. "We'd better go before the morning becomes the afternoon and we can't swim because the day has flown by," Adam said.

They scooted their chairs back and rose. Pat walked with them to the door and said goodbye.

As Shauna and Adam left the building and headed for Adam's Mercedes coupe parked in front of the building, Shauna said, "Pat is a jewel. How long has she been working for your family?"

"Ever since she dropped out of high school during the Depression. A few years ago I moved her to this apartment so she wouldn't have to work as hard. She wouldn't hear of retiring, and when she worked at the house as my housekeeper, she would work from sunup to sundown nonstop. The doctors told her to slow down, but not my Pat. Very few people stay in this apartment, so she has it to herself most of the time."

Shauna opened the car door and cocked her head to one side. "Then why me?"

"Because if I didn't send some people to stay there, she would storm into my office and demand to be taken back to the house." Adam shrugged. "Besides, I knew you two would hit it off great. She *is* a jewel and I don't want anything to happen to her because of her stubborn pride."

Shauna sat in the front seat and watched as Adam swung the car into the stream of traffic. They drove to his house in silence with Shauna recalling the trip the night before. Then her anger had blurred her vision of the green countryside with its vivid wild flowers, of the cattle and horses grazing, and the vastness of the land that stretched as far as the eye could see. But today she absorbed it all.

When Adam pulled into the long lane leading to his house, Shauna's muscles grew taut, her nerves raw. What if Veronica is there? she wondered, back from Houston early. I don't think I can face that woman again. I want Adam to myself for at least this one day. She will have him the rest of her life. Tears misted her eyes. Enjoy the time you have with him, she told herself, and scrambled from the car when Adam stopped in front of his house.

"I have quite a selection of swimsuits in the cabana by the pool. Take whichever one you want."

"Do you always keep ladies' suits on hand?"

Adam guided her through the house and into the garden. "Yes"—he looked down at her—"because I never know when I'll be able to persuade a beautiful woman to come home with me and swim. I don't want her to say she can't because she has no swimsuit. So I stock my cabana with several different sizes." He waved his arm. "No problem. No excuses."

"I can't imagine very many women turning you down, Adam. Pat is right. You can be very persuasive when you want to be."

He halted and bowed, sweeping his arm across his body, "Why thank ye, ma'am. I try to be."

Laughter bubbled from Shauna's throat. She opened the door and stepped inside the cabana, the sound of her amusement still floating in the air.

After quickly slipping into a one-piece black bathing suit with turquoise, white, and green stripes slanted diagonally across the front, Shauna walked from the cabana to sit by the side of the pool. She dangled her feet over the edge and recoiled at the cold bite to her skin.

Adam approached and sat next to her. He placed his feet in the water and splashed them.

"I thought you said it was heated."

He looked at Shauna and said, "It is, but I don't keep it the temperature of a bath. You would shrivel up in five minutes if I did."

Shauna eased her feet again into the water, one inch at a time, until half the calves of her legs were covered. Slowly she became accustomed to the coolness of the water and leaned her head back to let the sun warm her face.

"It is lovely here, Adam. You must swim every day. I would if I had a pool."

She heard his sigh and opened her eyes halfway. She studied him as he swam a few feet from her, his graceful movements mesmerizing her with the long, even strokes.

He called from the water, "I wish I could enjoy the pool more, but, alas, work beckons me more than I wish at times."

She fixed her gaze upon Adam and said, "I have seen

your books and know that you, Adam Steele, do not have to work so hard. You have plenty of money to just sit back and rest for a while. You don't want to be like Pat, do you?"

"But I have responsibilities to others that I can't forget so easily, Shauna. My work is important to me like yours is to you."

"Oh, you are impossible to reason with." Shauna rose to her feet. "I don't even know why you are here now. You should be at your office slaving over some contract or . . ." She dove into the water, the coolness washing over her. She surfaced next to Adam and continued, "Or working on a new project to bring you more millions."

He reached out and pushed Shauna's head into the water. She shoved him away and swam for the deep end.

When she broke through the surface again at the other end of the pool, she heard Adam's robust laughter. "Are you sure you can allow yourself this day to relax?" She taunted him with her question.

He laughed. "I'll have to remember next time to dunk your head with more force to stop that nagging tongue of yours."

Adam disappeared under the water. Her gaze followed his movements as he neared her. Gripping the ledge of the pool, she held on for dear life when his hand grabbed her legs. Her hands began to slip from the edge. Her fingernails dug into the stone, but second by second she lost her ground until she plunged to the bottom as Adam dragged her down. He caught her in his viselike hold and crushed her to him. His lips pressed into hers as they slowly rose to the top. For a brief second she relished the feel of his lips on hers. Then the doubts came.

He's engaged. Don't let him hurt you any more than he has, Shauna told herself.

As the cool air enveloped Shauna, she swam away from Adam and gasped for breath. Her cheeks flamed as her body became a mass of chills. She ran her fingers over her mouth and just stared at Adam for a long moment, each of them trapped within the other's gaze.

The coldness seeped into Shauna's thoughts and she blinked to break the spell that held her to him. She dove through the water and made her way to the other side of the pool, where she pulled herself up onto the stone ledge and grabbed a towel. Adam swam ten laps with quick, energetic strokes, then stepped out of the pool. Without a word, he took his towel and strode to the cabana. Her gaze sought the place where Adam had kissed her only moments before.

Why? she asked herself. I don't understand him. I don't understand myself. Why?

She rested her head on her knees and closed her eyes, listening to the sounds of the garden, the birds chirping, the leaves rustling in the gentle breeze. Shauna felt herself drifting into a dream world, where Adam embraced her with his strong arms, his mouth imprisoning hers. She saw herself lying next to him, her head upon his chest. Then a face loomed near Shauna, the green eyes flashing their hatred and warning. Shauna flinched from the piercing intensity of the features that glared at her from Veronica's face.

A hand touched her and Shauna snapped open her eyes and stared into Adam's face.

"Shauna, you'd better get dressed now. I don't want you to get sick."

She lifted her head from her knees and rose. "Perhaps that would be the best thing that could happen. Then you'd be forced to get yourself someone else to work on your tax statements with your accountants. Let me return to New Orleans where I belong."

A cloud passed over Adam's face, then quickly vanished before Shauna could tell what had captured his gaze. "No! Don't talk like that!" Then in a quieter voice he added, "You've been telling me what a good lawyer you are. Then save me some money and I'll acknowledge that fact, but not until then. Prove to me that a woman can work as well as a man." Amusement masked the earlier emotion, his eyes dancing with merriment. He turned Shauna around and gave her a gentle slap on the bottom. "Now get dressed before you turn blue."

Shauna shot him a look over her shoulder. "I'm not so sure you're kidding, Adam. I *can* do as good a job as any man and better than most."

She hurried to the cabana and dressed in her jeans and T-shirt. When she reappeared outside by the pool, a table was set with food already on the plates. Adam rose to pull a chair out for her and she sank into its softness.

"I hope you like your steak medium rare. I noticed last night that was what you ordered."

Shauna arched a brow. "Very observant." She took her knife and cut a thick piece of her T-bone steak.

Glancing at Adam, she caught him staring at her. A smile spread across his mouth, lighting his eyes. "You do like to eat." A laugh escaped his lips. "I haven't seen anyone as small as you enjoy food as much as you do. Veronica is constantly dieting."

Shauna's eyes narrowed in a frown. She stiffened at the mention of Veronica and lowered her gaze as she pushed her peas around her plate with her fork. "I've never had to worry about my weight like some people do," she murmured.

"Tell me, what do you think of Veronica?"

Shauna raised her head up and, with her eyes wide, stared at Adam. His lips were tightly drawn, his eyes void of all expression.

Shauna studied her plate and searched her mind for the right reply. She stammered, "I . . . I . . . don't know . . . her."

"Shauna, I know you have formed an opinion by the way you are gripping your fork. You don't have to tell me what you think about her, because I can tell by your actions and silence. Veronica is from my world. We grew up together. Ever since I can remember our parents have wanted us to marry. When my parents were killed in a plane crash three years ago, I made a vow to myself that I would carry out that wish for them. I need an heir and she seems as good a choice as any for a wife."

"Three years ago! Why did you wait so long?" Shauna regretted her question the second she spoke it and chewed on her bottom lip as she watched Adam try to find the answer to her question.

He shook his head. "I never seemed to find the time to propose. When my father died, I had to take over the business, and that was quite an undertaking. And I suppose in a way I took Veronica for granted. She never hid how she felt about me."

Shauna clenched the napkin in her lap. In a whisper she asked, "And how do you feel about her?"

Silence.

Shauna lifted her head and through a curtain of lashes saw Adam's clouded features. She buried her fingernails into the material of the napkin.

When Adam's reply came, Shauna leaned closer to him to hear the whispered answer. "I don't know anymore."

Shauna caught her bottom lip between her teeth as she listened to the anguish that his words held.

"I'm sorry. It wasn't my place to ask."

He ignored her words and continued, "Shauna, I used to think that Veronica and I suited one another. We come from the same background, believe in the same things, but now I find myself questioning my feelings about her."

He slammed his fist into the table. The dishes rattled. Shauna's eyes grew rounder as his face contorted with his indecision.

"Something is missing and I don't know what." He fell silent and stared across the pool. Suddenly he bolted to his feet and said in a harsh voice, "I think it's time for me to take you back to the apartment."

Shauna rose and took a step forward. With each step she felt the heaviness weigh her down until she thought she wouldn't be able to move. Her lungs ached. Her eyes burned from the unshed tears that brimmed in them. As Shauna followed Adam and saw his rigidly set jaw and the ramrod-straight back, she screamed within her mind, You can't marry her! Can't you see that?

*But he isn't a man to go back on his word, Shauna,* an inner voice said.

I know, she thought. He will keep that promise.

# Chapter Twelve

Shauna pushed back her chair. "Well, that seems to take care of that section, Mr. Ripley."

"Please call me Tom. You make me sound so old when you say Mr. Ripley."

Shauna smiled. "Well, I for one am glad it is time to go home. I'm beat."

"I believe Monday is the worst day of the week. You know you have four more days in this work week to go. You'd think people would be rested and ready to go on Monday, but most people around here just drag themselves through the day." Tom stood and walked with Shauna to the door. "Especially after that party Thursday night and the long weekend. Did you enjoy your first weekend in Dallas? There is a lot to see if you have never been here."

"My weekend was very quiet. I spent the time resting—something I hadn't done in a while." Shauna opened the door and stepped forward. Over her shoulder she said, "I'll take this report to Mr. Steele's office."

"It can wait until tomorrow. Mr. Steele flew to Houston yesterday and won't be back until tomorrow afternoon."

Shauna clutched the paper tighter and shrugged. "Oh, well, if that is the case then he won't need these figures now." She handed the report to Tom and left the office.

As Shauna rode the elevator to the ground floor, an overwhelming depression overcame her. He went to see her, she thought. Veronica was only gone a few days and he just had to see her. Well, he certainly cares more for her than his business if he just picks up and flies to her whenever she wants him.

Shauna walked from the building, her mind raging with her thoughts. I don't care about him. Whatever made me think I cared?

*Don't kid yourself, Shauna. You care. You will always care, but you must face the fact that he will marry Veronica in a few months,* an inner voice said.

Shauna forced the key into the ignition of her company car and backed out of her parking space. As she clutched the wheel, she tried to calm herself. But when she parked her car in the garage of her apartment building, she still seethed, her hands aching from the tight grip she had had on the steering wheel.

"Pat, I'm home," she called out when she strode into the apartment.

Pat emerged from the kitchen with a smile plastered

178

on her face. "Shauna, I've been waiting all day for you to come home. A package arrived for you from a florist." She handed her a long box.

Shauna lay her purse on the entrance hall table and started to open the box with trembling hands. She slipped the large yellow ribbon from the box and lifted the lid.

Her eyes widened and she gasped as she dropped the box. A long-stemmed black rose fell from the box, a horrible odor filling the air. Shauna stood rooted to the spot, staring at the rose lying at her feet.

Pat picked up the rose and shook her head. "Who would send you something like this?" She walked to the wastebasket and dumped the flower into it. "Well, I wouldn't worry about it. Just a little joke, that's all." She forced a cheerful tone into her voice as she continued, "Now what time do you want dinner? I'm fixing you my special casserole."

Shauna heard Pat's question, but no words would form in her throat. "A warning," she whispered finally.

"A warning, my child?"

Shauna lifted her gaze to meet Pat's. "A warning!" Her voice grew shrill. "She is warning me to leave him alone."

"Who is warning you, Shauna?" Pat moved next to Shauna and touched her arm. "I think you'd better sit down. You look pale."

Shauna stooped and searched the box for a card. "She didn't even have the nerve to send me a card with this . . . this gift."

"Who are you talking about?"

Shauna stood and looked at Pat. "Veronica Blake!"

Pat placed her arm around Shauna's shoulder and said in a soft voice, "Child, let's go into the kitchen and talk. I think you need someone to listen to you."

Tears choked Shauna's throat and filled her eyes. She blinked and they spilled onto her cheeks. Pat handed her a tissue and Shauna patted her cheeks dry.

She sniffled and said, "I think you're right, Pat, I'm so miserable." Shauna swallowed hard. "What am I going to do?" She heard the desperate plea in her voice, but a heaviness around her heart lessened as she spoke to Pat.

Pat guided her into the kitchen and sat her in a chair at the table.

"Now tell me where you met Adam Steele. I could tell you knew him before coming to Dallas last week."

Shauna dropped her gaze to the floor and ran her finger along the edge of the table. "I met him while he was on a cruise last month. We . . . we became friends . . . good friends."

Pat released a breath of air. "Oh, I see. That isn't like Adam to lead someone on. He is a very straightforward man—direct, honest, formal. You can thank his parents for that. I think he is even a bit stuffy at times. He doesn't know how to sit back and enjoy himself very well. Not much practice with that when he was growing up. Do you know he went to work for his father at the age of fourteen?" Pat leaned closer to Shauna. "He has worked in every department of his company over the last twenty years. His father wanted him to know every operation of the business, so consequently the child didn't learn to play." Pat's face screwed into a frown.

Shauna watched the frown deepen as Pat searched

her memory. "I love him, Pat. I don't want him to marry someone like Veronica. She's no good for him." Shauna's voice cracked as her tears returned to flow down her cheeks.

Pat gathered Shauna into her arms and held Shauna as she cried. "The ties between Adam and Miss Blake go back a long time," Pat said. "I wish I could give you hope, but I can't. Once Adam makes up his mind he rarely changes it. He has always weighed every side of an issue, then decided after he has examined all possibilities."

Shauna drew back and stared at Pat. "Do you know what you are saying? He sounds like a computer."

"But Adam operates like one. He isn't a man to make a rash decision. That's why he doesn't change his mind often."

"What kind of life is that?" Shauna flew to her feet and began to pace the floor. "And a woman like Veronica will settle for a man like that?"

"Aren't you willing *to settle for a man like that,* as you say it? He has a lot to offer a woman like Veronica Blake. He is handsome, rich, powerful, appealing . . ."

Shauna whirled and faced Pat. "Enough! I know what he is." Shauna headed for the door. She glanced back at Pat and said, "I'm not hungry. I think I'll retire early. Good night."

Shauna saw the sad and hurt expression that washed over Pat's face, the slow shake of Pat's head. Unshed tears glistened in Shauna's eyes. Her pace quickened as she fled from the kitchen to the safety of her room.

Shauna paced the floor of her bedroom. "I shouldn't let Veronica affect me so much. She's trying to protect her future. I need this job." She stood by the bedpost and gripped it, breathing deeply.

She turned at the sound of the bedroom door opening and froze as she watched Veronica enter the room.

"How did you get in here?" Shauna asked.

"Through the front door, my dear. I see you received my gift." She smiled, slivers of ice in her eyes.

"You can't frighten me, Veronica. It's a waste of your time."

Veronica tossed back her head and laughed. "You're so naive. Such an innocent. You're still a virgin, no doubt. I'm sure that's why Adam is intrigued by you. You're a challenge to his male ego. But how long do you think that will last when he has gotten you in bed? You may become his mistress after we're married, but I'll be his wife, the mother of his children." Veronica fingered her engagement ring. "He'll tire of you like all the rest. He always comes back to me. We understand each other."

Shauna moved forward. "Get out! This is still my apartment." The trembling began in the hands and spread until her whole body quivered with rage.

Veronica shrugged. "Suit yourself. I tried to warn you."

When Veronica closed the door behind her, Shauna threw herself on the bed and pounded her fists into the mattress. Sobs racked her body. I'm leaving, came the thought. I can't stay here and torture myself another day.

Shauna scrambled off the bed and extracted her suitcases from the closet. She began to stuff her clothes into them. *Mistress!* snowballed through her mind as she packed.

The phone on Mr. Ripley's desk rang. He picked it up and said, "Yes, Tom Ripley here."

Shauna concentrated on the column of numbers on the paper before her and ignored the rest of the conversation. When she heard the receiver being placed in its cradle, she looked up and raised one eyebrow.

"Mr. Steele wants to see you now in his office. That was his secretary on the phone."

Shauna put her pencil down and stood. "Good. I was going to stop by on the way home tonight to have a talk with him, but now is as good a time as any."

Shauna's heart raced with the anticipation of seeing Adam one more time before returning to New Orleans. She could remember debating the night before over whether or not to give her resignation in person. He deserves at least that. I won't be like Mark and send a letter, she thought, and stepped into Adam's outer office.

His secretary escorted her into his office, then left Shauna standing in front of Adam's desk. He glanced up from the paper he was reading and waved her to be seated.

Shauna saw his face light with a smile that made his eyes sparkle. Her lungs constricted, the words she had been going to say to him flying from her mind. She stared at him and waited, a numbness encasing her.

He rose, walked from behind the desk, and sat in the chair next to her.

"I'm going back to New Orleans, Adam. I don't want to be your lawyer. In fact, I think it's better if I never see you again."

"What's happened? I thought that you cared for me. That . . ."

"Whatever you thought is wrong, Adam." She rose and put some distance between them. "I could never be a man's mistress." She looked out the window. "Never, Adam."

"Mistress? What do you mean?" His voice sounded harsh.

Shauna turned, at a loss for words. "Well . . . er . . . Veronica told me . . ."

His frown dissolved. "Veronica!" He crossed the room and grasped her hands within his. "Shauna, I couldn't wait to return to Dallas to see *you,*" he said in a gentle voice that made Shauna shiver.

Her eyes grew wide.

"I went to Houston to talk with Veronica about our relationship. After talking with you on Friday, I knew that I couldn't marry her. I knew the marriage would never last because *I love you.*"

Shauna felt her heart hammer against her chest. "Love me?"

He cupped her chin in his hands and leaned toward her to kiss her. The gentle pressure of his lips sent a tremor streaking through her. His hand moved to rake its fingers through her hair and the other one to mold her to him.

"Yes, darling. I love you and have for a long time. I just never knew what these feelings were until Friday. I want to marry *you,* not Veronica."

"What did she say about that? I imagine Veronica

didn't care too much for the idea." Shauna cuddled closer and listened to Adam's galloping heartbeat.

He laughed. "Yes, you're right about that. She was furious. She said she would sue me for breach of contract. I told her to go ahead, but that it wouldn't change my mind. I have an excellent lawyer to represent me."

Shauna traced a pattern along Adam's hand. "Are you sure about this? You and Veronica are so alike."

He pulled away. "I'm not sure I like that. Lately I've seen Veronica in a different light. What I see isn't to my liking."

Shauna smiled. "I mean you come from the same background, the same lifestyle. We are so different."

"I know you make me feel good. I've always worked so hard and played so little. I need someone to show me that life won't be a round of business dinners and formal parties. You're good for me. You help me to relax." Adam brushed a tendril of hair from Shauna's cheek. "I'll enjoy getting to know everything about you. You're such a delight. I don't think I'll ever forget when you came to my dinner party dressed to clean the house."

Shauna wiggled from Adam's embrace. "Dressed to clean your house!" She inhaled deeply then exhaled through pursed lips. "I'll have you know that what I wore to your stuffy party was perfectly suited for most affairs."

"For most, but not a formal dinner party."

"Why, Adam Steele, don't talk to me about clothes. If you would wear more comfortable clothes some of the time, you'd look a lot better than always wearing those three-piece suits." Shauna started toward the door. Halfway across the office Adam grabbed her and spun her around. She fell against his chest, his arms drawing her against him.

He whispered into her ear, "And such a fiery temper."

She tilted back her head and looked him in the eye. "And you just remember that when you insult me in the future, if you're brave enough to."

He caressed her with his lips, kissing her eyelids, the tip of her nose, then her mouth. Their lips joined in a kiss that deepened and left Shauna breathless. Her muscles felt like liquid as she leaned into Adam. He ran his hand up and down her back, massaging her.

"Adam, I can't believe this is happening to me. I never dreamed we'd fall in love with each other. How? Why?"

He kissed her forehead and laughed. "As I said before, you're a delight, darling. How? Why?" Adam shrugged. "Why do two people fall in love in the first place? Some kind of magical ingredient between them, I suppose."

Shauna lay her head on Adam's chest and felt the rapid rise and fall of his chest. "Well, I'm thankful for magical ingredients."

"Well, well, if that isn't the sweetest scene I've pictured in a long time."

Shauna turned around to see Veronica enter the office with Adam's secretary trailing behind her.

"I'm sorry, Mr. Steele. She just barged right past me," the secretary said.

"That's all right, Mrs. Jackson. You may leave now."

When the door closed, Adam turned on Veronica and

said in a too-quiet voice, "What are you doing here? I thought we said all we needed to already."

Veronica advanced into the center of the office. She removed her leather gloves and put them in her purse. "Not quite, my dear." Veronica's gaze flickered over Shauna. "I see you couldn't wait to get home to her. I certainly don't think much of a woman who steals another's fiancé."

Shauna backed away from Adam and took several steps toward Veronica, her hands clenched at her sides.

"Leave, Veronica, before I do something I'll regret," Adam said.

"No, Adam. I have something to say to Miss Blake." Shauna moved forward and halted in front of Veronica. Shauna's forehead creased with a frown and her eyes narrowed to two slits, the fury of a storm in their depths. "And what I have to say won't take long. I don't want you ever to threaten me again. Your black rose didn't do the trick." Shauna stepped forward as Veronica backed away. "And don't you ever come around Adam or me again. Now leave before *I* throw you out!"

Veronica huffed in anger. "I never." Her gaze darted from Shauna to Adam and back to Shauna.

Shauna took a step closer to Veronica. Veronica twisted around, yanked open the door, and hurried from the office.

"If I ever need someone to do battle for me, I think I've found that person. You're a little spitfire, my love. Remind me never to get on your wrong side." Adam pulled Shauna to him.

She lifted her gaze to the love mirrored in his eyes. "I

love you, Adam Steele." She stood on tiptoes and planted a kiss on his mouth.

He hugged her and swung her around. "Baby, what fun we're going to have!"

"Promise?" Shauna ran her fingers through his hair, pulled his head toward hers, and met his lips in a kiss.

# Silhouette Romance

## ROMANCE THE WAY
## IT USED TO BE...
## AND COULD BE AGAIN

*Contemporary romances for today's women.*
*Each month, six very special love stories will be yours*
*from SILHOUETTE.*
*Look for them wherever books are sold*
*or order now from the coupon below.*

$1.50 each

# Silhouette Romance

___ #49 DANCER IN THE SHADOWS Wisdom
___ #50 DUSKY ROSE Scott
___ #51 BRIDE OF THE SUN Hunter
___ #52 MAN WITHOUT A HEART Hampson
___ #53 CHANCE TOMORROW Browning
___ #54 LOUISIANA LADY Beckman
___ #55 WINTER'S HEART Ladame
___ #56 RISING STAR Trent
___ #57 TO TRUST TOMORROW John
___ #58 LONG WINTER'S NIGHT Stanford
___ #59 KISSED BY MOONLIGHT Vernon
___ #60 GREEN PARADISE Hill
___ #61 WHISPER MY NAME Michaels
___ #62 STAND-IN BRIDE Halston

___ #63 SNOWFLAKES IN THE SUN Brent
___ #64 SHADOW OF APOLLO Hampson
___ #65 A TOUCH OF MAGIC Hunter
___ #66 PROMISES FROM THE PAST Vitek
___ #67 ISLAND CONQUEST Hastings
___ #68 THE MARRIAGE BARGAIN Scott
___ #69 WEST OF THE MOON St. George
___ #70 MADE FOR EACH OTHER Afton Bonds
___ #71 A SECOND CHANCE ON LOVE Ripy
___ #72 ANGRY LOVER Beckman
___ #73 WREN OF PARADISE Browning
___ #74 WINTER DREAMS Trent
___ #75 DIVIDE THE WIND Carroll

## Coming in June From Silhouette

# JANET DAILEY'S
# THE HOSTAGE BRIDE

-------------------------------------------

**SILHOUETTE BOOKS, Department SB/1**
1230 Avenue of the Americas
New York, NY 10020

Please send me the books I have checked above. I am enclosing $_____ (please add 50¢ to cover postage and handling. NYS and NYC residents please add appropriate sales tax). Send check or money order—no cash or C.O.D.'s please. Allow six weeks for delivery.

NAME_____

ADDRESS_____

CITY_____ STATE/ZIP_____

*Silhouette Romance*

# 15-Day Free Trial Offer
# 6 Silhouette Romances

**6 Silhouette Romances, free for 15 days!** We'll send you 6 new Silhouette Romances to keep for 15 days, absolutely free! If you decide not to keep them, send them back to us. We'll pay the return postage. You pay nothing.

**Free Home Delivery.** But if you enjoy them as much as we think you will, keep them by paying us the retail price of just $1.50 each. We'll pay all shipping and handling charges. You'll then automatically become a member of the Silhouette Book Club, and will receive 6 more new Silhouette Romances every month and a bill for $9.00. That's the same price you'd pay in the store, but you get the convenience of home delivery.

**Read every book we publish.** The Silhouette Book Club is the way to make sure you'll be able to receive every new romance we publish.

This offer expires October 31, 1981

Silhouette Book Club, Dept. SBC17B
120 Brighton Road, Clifton, NJ 07012

Please send me 6 Silhouette Romances to keep for 15 days, absolutely free. I understand I am not obligated to join the Silhouette Book Club unless I decide to keep them.

NAME_____

ADDRESS_____

CITY_____STATE_____ZIP_____

# READERS' COMMENTS ON SILHOUETTE ROMANCES:

"You give us joy and surprises throughout the books . . . they're the best books I've read."
—J.S.*, Crosby, MN

"Needless to say I am addicted to your books. . . . I love the characters, the settings, the emotions."
—V.D., Plane, TX

"Every one was written with the utmost care. The story of each captures one's interest early in the plot and holds it through until the end."
—P.B., Summersville, WV

"I get so carried away with the books I forget the time."
—L.W., Beltsville, MD

"Silhouette has a great talent for picking winners."
—K.W., Detroit, MI

* names available on request.